# SECRET CINCINNATI

## A GUIDE TO THE WEIRD, WONDERFUL, AND OBSCURE

Kathryn Witt

Reedy Press
PO Box 5131
St. Louis, MO 63139
www.reedypress.com



Library of Congress Control Number: 2018945705

ISBN: 9781681061870

Design by Jill Halpin

Photography by John Witt.

Printed in the United States of America
19 20 21 22 5 4 3 2

For Sam and Krysta

# CONTENTS

## ACKNOWLEDGMENTS

Any book about secrets revealed necessarily requires an able assist from willing blabber-mouths, and I had *lots* of help in that department.

Everywhere I went, someone would let me slip behind the curtain and learn the story. Especially enthusiastic and generous with their time and assistance were Laurie Risch and Sharen Kardon of Behringer-Crawford Museum, Cathy Collopy of Dinsmore Homestead, Tricia Watts of Gorman Heritage Farm, Leland Hite and Larry Moster of Greater Cincinnati Water Works, Richard Watson of Mary M. Emery Memorial Carillon, and Stephen Enzweiler of St. Mary's Cathedral Basilica of the Assumption, as well as the folks at Great Parks of Hamilton County and the Boar's Head and Yule Log Festival. To each, I am truly thankful for help, insights, and the extra mile received.

Graciously letting the cat out of the bag about a number of under-the-radar places and spaces were Frankie Kropp, Becky Linhardt, Deb Pittman, Elizabeth Robinson, Krysta Wilham, Sam Witt, and a gaggle of great minds at the Kenton County Public Library. Your leads were very much appreciated.

Joining in on many of the adventures all over Greater Cincinnati/Northern Kentucky was my mom, Helen Lentz, who had her own insights to share, and a pint-sized researcher, Simon Jetton Stotts, who was disappointed about the ghost ship but rallied for the ferry.

*Photo courtesy of John Witt.*

# INTRODUCTION

For those who grew up in the Greater Cincinnati/Northern Kentucky area, it may be hard to believe there are any secrets that haven't already been uncovered somewhere along the journey. Yet we pass parks, buildings, cemeteries, monuments, and hidden treasures every day that we don't really take notice of or, if we do, we don't stop and wonder.

Why?

Why is that there? What forces combined to put it where it is? What is the history behind it? Who lived there? Died here? Who (or what) is buried beneath the ground?

What's the story?

While crisscrossing the city, I found much to marvel at, from the original mission of one of the area's key cultural hubs, which took a dip into the occult, and a gourmand's spice palace where the names of dozens of seasonings contort the tongue, to a statue with an identity complex and a tour whose destination is a mystery to the daredevils who willingly lay down some serious cash to be on it.

Buried beer history. A play on *Pulp Fiction*. Carved and colorful masks. A secret, showy garden. Discoveries await beneath the ground, behind closed doors, inside glass cases, and around the next bend in the road.

In spite of living and working here, Greater Cincinnati/Northern Kentucky had plenty of secrets up her sleeve to share with me. And I had a wonderful time going behind the scenes, uncovering the mysteries, learning the history, and hearing the stories.

I hope you enjoy unearthing all that is strange, surprising, and sensational in Greater Cincinnati/Northern Kentucky. It truly is a place of wonder.

# 1 ABRAHAM LINCOLN STATUE

### Why is Cincinnati's statue of Honest Abe so, well, ugly?

Having been born in 1809 on the rough-and-tumble Kentucky frontier, where he spent the first seven years of his life, it might not come as a surprise that at least one statue depicts the sixteenth president with wildly tousled hair and in wrinkled clothing with shirt collar askew. What is startling, as some have historically argued, is the grotesqueness of it.

Ironically, the statue rises from one of the most picturesque parks in Cincinnati. Lytle Park is tucked into the Lytle Park Historic District in a quiet corner of the central business district. Known for its dramatic and colorful floral displays that change with the season, the tiny park is a scenic stroll from the Taft Museum of Art, although the statue is not looking toward the museum, but away, and with an unbearded visage marked by furrowed brow and stern mouth.

In 1912 or so, the Charles P. Taft family (Charles was the brother of President William Howard Taft) commissioned artist George Grey Barnard to create the Lincoln statue. As much a pioneer in sculpting as the Great Emancipator was himself in so many disciplines, Barnard studied Lincoln's life masks (molds taken from living faces) to create his sculpture.

---

The statue is a short walk from the Taft Museum of Art, the home of Anna Sinton and Charles Phelps Taft from 1873–1929. President William Howard Taft accepted his presidential nomination from the home's portico in 1908.

## ABRAHAM LINCOLN STATUE

**WHAT** Ugly statue of President Lincoln

**WHERE** 501 E. Fourth St.

**COST** Free

**PRO TIP** Visit the park in springtime to see a profusion of colorful tulips in bloom.

cincinnatiparks.com

*The Abraham Lincoln statue was dedicated in 1917 by former US President William Howard Taft. Photo courtesy of John Witt.*

The end result? A raw and unsentimental sculpt showing every line and facial fissure.

One can almost hear the collective gasp of shock and disapproval that rose from the crowd at its 1917 unveiling. Here is a face only a mother could love. The statue was proclaimed hideous by some, downright disrespectful to so beloved a president by others.

Still, the statue remains a proud fixture in the park built by Civil War General William Henry Lytle and surrounded by manicured swatches of lawn, crabapple trees, benches, and lampposts. Curiously, it is on the original site of the Lytle family homestead, built by Lytle's grandfather the same year Lincoln was born.

# 2 *GARDEN PARTY AT THE TAFT* MURAL

**Why is a mural celebrating masterpieces from a Cincinnati art museum painted on a flower shop in Bellevue?**

Stroll along the avenue—Fairfield Avenue, that is—in Bellevue, Kentucky, and you will come across a lavishly colorful and captivating mural depicting a scene of guests enjoying themselves outdoors. Splashed across a building located in the 200 block of the Historic Fairfield Avenue Business District, the mural actually portrays subjects from a handful of masterpieces that hang on the walls inside the Taft Museum of Art, a historic house museum in Cincinnati.

*Garden Party at the Taft* suggests exactly that, with a couple lounging on a blanket on the lawn, a woman entertaining her companions with music, a mother cuddling her baby, a fashionable gent looking as though he's staring right at you and about to greet you, even a pair of lazy dogs. The ornateness of the Taft Museum shows in the background; beautiful pink peony blossoms dominate the foreground. Adding a touch of the fantastical is a demon bursting forth from a tree and riding a lion.

Featured masterpieces include Rembrandt Van Rijn's *Portrait of a Man Rising from his Chair, The Song of the Talking Wire* by Henry F. Farny, *World of Their Own* by Lawrence Alma Tadema, *Edward and William Tomkinson* by Thomas

---

See the original works depicted in the mural at the Taft Museum of Art in Cincinnati. All are part of the museum's permanent collection and on view.

*Get a taste of the Taft Museum of Art with a stroll through Bellevue, KY. Photo courtesy of John Witt.*

Gainsborough, and *Mrs. John Weyland and her Son John* by Joshua Reynolds. The demon and lion figure are from a Chinese vase dating to the Qing dynasty (early eighteenth century) and depicts an episode from the fourteenth-century historical novel *Romance of the Three Kingdoms*.

The mural was created in 2012 by the award-winning ArtWorks, a non-profit organization that employs and trains local youth and talent to create art and community impact, in partnership with the Taft Museum of Art. It was part of the museum's Eightieth Anniversary Celebration, "Art for All."

## GARDEN PARTY AT THE TAFT

**WHAT** Mural of masterpieces

**WHERE** Petri's Flowers Building, 229 Fairfield Ave., Bellevue, KY

**COST** Free

**PRO TIP** Fairfield Ave. is filled with a variety of shops and restaurants in architecturally beautiful nineteenth-century storefronts.

# 3 CAREW TOWER OBSERVATION DECK

**What venue that is part of a fabled city view also presents a fabled city view?**

You've appreciated the building's beauty from various vantage points around the city when oohing and ahhing over Cincinnati's storied skyline, but have you gone up to the forty-ninth floor of the Carew Tower to check out the view from its Observation Deck?

Cincinnati's tallest building until the Great American Tower, crowned with its lattice-like bishop's mitre, bumped it back to second, this National Historic Landmark is still the highest elevated building.

It soared into the skyline in the heart of downtown in 1930, an homage to the Art Deco style taking the country's architectural landscape by storm. It verily screamed glamour and sophistication.

Designed to be a city within a city, a new concept at the time, it was (and is) home to offices, restaurants, a distinctive

## CAREW TOWER OBSERVATION DECK

**WHAT** A decked out view

**WHERE** 41 W. Fifth St.

**COST** $4 ages twelve and up; $2 ages six-eleven; free for ages five and under.

**PRO TIP** Bring cash; credit cards and checks are not accepted.

facebook.com/carewtower

Carew Tower takes its name from Joseph Carew of Mabley & Carew department store chain fame. Founded in 1877, Mabley & Carew was located in Carew Tower when it opened in 1930.

(Above) *It's up, up and away with a ride to the Observation Deck at the Carew Tower.* (Left) *See the beautiful Art Deco color that flourishes inside the Carew Tower. Photos courtesy of John Witt.*

collection of shops, and the Hilton Cincinnati Netherland Plaza (formerly the Omni Netherland Plaza), itself a rich example of French Art Deco architecture, which opened a year later in 1931.

Slip into the building's revolving door, follow the lobby signs to the Observation Deck elevator, and whoosh up to the forty-fifth floor in a matter of seconds. From here, it's a fork-in-the-road option: You can either walk up the remaining four flights of stairs or squeeze into a four-person elevator and ride up to the forty-eighth floor, then climb the staircase to the forty-ninth.

Either way, prepare to be blown away when you step through the door to the Observation Deck. Here is the holy grail of views, a 360-degree panorama that sweeps around the city, taking in the Ohio River, the six bridges spanning it, deep into northern Kentucky, the office buildings that give way to patches of green, and the residential communities surrounding downtown Cincinnati.

It is a million-dollar view that costs only four, and it is worth every single greenback.

# 4 COLONEL DE GOURMET HERBS & SPICES

## Where can you find asafetida and other unpronounceable and exotic herbs and spices?

Spot the mustachioed mister in the white jacket and string tie rummaging among the six hundred to seven hundred spices and blends at Findlay Market and another similarly dapper gent springs to mind.

There's a reason Colonel De looks like he's channeling Colonel Sanders, the fried chicken titan whose eleven secret herb and spice blend has risen to near mythological heights: He worked for Sanders (twice) and learned a lot about marketing and the mystery of spices. He also attended the same church as Sanders.

The reigning herb and spice guy, known simply as the Colonel, is De Stewart, owner of Colonel De Gourmet Herbs & Spices. He has been a fixture at Findlay Market, Ohio's oldest continuously operated public market (having opened in 1852) and beloved Cincinnati institution, since 2006. And he has to have hundreds of spices stocked in generous quantities; the market welcomes more than one million visitors every year.

*Find Apocalypse (so hot it should "come with a release") and Zahtar, which flavors meats and veggies and everything in between. Baby Carter's Sweet Butt & Booty Rub is versatile*

---

Most people have no idea that when they dine out at Greater Cincinnati restaurants they are most likely eating Colonel De's spices. The spice empire supplies about sixty restaurants locally and across the country.

*The mustachioed Colonel De waits on customers at his Findlay Market store.Photo courtesy of John Witt.*

## COLONEL DE GOURMET HERBS & SPICES

**WHAT** Herbs and spices from A to Z

**WHERE** Findlay Market, 1801 Race St., Jungle Jim's Eastgate; 4450 Eastgate South Dr.; and Fort Thomas World Headquarters, 18 N. Fort Thomas Ave., Fort Thomas, KY

**COST** Browsing is free. Spices and blends by the ounce range from $.46 (salt) to $249 (saffron).

**PRO TIP** How do you use baharat, quassia bark, or epizote? Colonel De's staff can advise on the different usages of each product.

colonelde.com

*and fun to say. The Colonel's Bayou Blend takes you straight to Norleans.*

Khmeli Suneli is a traditional Georgian spicy herb mixture. Ras El Hanout is a North African blend of thirty-five spices. Asafetida subs in for onions or garlic for those with an allergy to allium.

The Colonel has two other locations as well; one at Jungle Jim's in Cincinnati's Eastgate neighborhood, and the other, the company's world headquarters, across the river in Fort Thomas. The storefront retail operation is joined by corporate offices, a warehouse, and a production facility. This is where the Colonel works his magic in creating both wet blends (marinades, sauces, soups) and dry mixes (protein rubs, herb and spice blends).

# 5 DAMASCUS ROOM

## How did a room built in Syria find its way to a museum's second-floor gallery?

Tucked way back in a corner on the second floor of the Cincinnati Art Museum is a stunning permanent exhibit comprising white marble floor tiles, gold-leafed panels, and European Baroque–inspired hand-painted geometric designs. Called the Damascus Room, it is considered one of the city's most treasured displays.

### DAMASCUS ROOM

**WHAT** Ancient, ornate parlor

**WHERE** Cincinnati Art Museum, 953 Eden Park Dr.

**COST** General admission and parking (in museum lot) are free. Cost for special exhibits varies; tickets may be purchased at cincinnatiartmuseum.org

**PRO TIP** The Damascus Room presents a dizzying and intricate array of designs, patterns, and architectural elements, so the explanatory chat cards are worth reading.

Andrew M. Jergens, founder of the Andrew Jergens Company, which was called the Jergens Soap Company when it was established in 1882, found the room in a Syrian home on a 1932 trip to the Middle East. Dating to the early eighteenth century, it is considered to be among the earliest surviving rooms from Syria.

The soap magnate purchased the room and relocated it to his private residence, a home built in the Richardsonian Romanesque style of the late nineteenth century in Cincinnati's Northside neighborhood. In its place of origin, likely located upstairs in the home, this ornately detailed room served as a reception parlor, where guests might be served tea and coffee. In the Jergens home, the Damascus Room was used as his library.

*Damascus Room, 1711-12, carved and gessoed wood with painted and decoration, Cincinnati Art Museum, Gift of Andrew N. Jergens, 1966.433*

According to Ainsley Cameron, Cincinnati Art Museum's Curator of South Asian Art, Islamic Art & Antiquities, the Damascus Room is one of only a handful of such rooms on display in US museums and academic institutions. Other examples are at the Metropolitan Museum in New York, the Cathedral of Learning at the University of Pittsburgh, and the Doris Duke Foundation for Islamic Art in Honolulu.

Lavishly decorated, elaborately furnished, and utterly priceless, the Damascus Room has an immersive quality and a quiet, contemplative atmosphere. Step inside this intimate space and experience embellishments typical of the Ottoman decorative style and featuring wall panels with inscriptions, floral adornments, and vignettes of a tranquil river landscape. Jergens gifted the room to the museum in 1966.

---

Does the Damascus Room give a glimpse into the interior décor of Jergens's private residence? We'll never know. Per Jergens's will, the house was demolished less than a year after his death in 1967.

# 6 FALCON THEATRE

**How did a thirty-year-old producing theatre become Cincinnati's only true storefront theatre?**

Tucked in the midst of Newport's Monmouth Street Historic District is the Falcon Theatre, founded in 1989 and known for bringing high-caliber theatrical productions to Cincinnati. This little theatre that could has been responsible for bringing such premieres to the area as *The Grapes of Wrath, Driving Miss Daisy, Poseidon: The Upside-Down Musical*, and *Gilligan's Island: The Musical.*

> **FALCON THEATRE**
>
> **WHAT** Storefront theatre
>
> **WHERE** 636 Monmouth St., Newport, KY
>
> **COST** $22 (tickets may be purchased online at falcontheater.net) .
>
> **PRO TIP** The Falcon Theatre building is a stop on American Legacy's Newport Gangster Tour. In Newport's "Sin City" heyday, it was La Madame's adult entertainment venue.

The old storefront this small, professional theatre company calls home is in one of Newport's most vibrant neighborhoods, a mix of architecturally beautiful residences, locally owned restaurants, and dynamic entertainment venues that give Newport's main commercial street its hustle-bustle verve. Many of the buildings date back to the 1850s, and it is no surprise that the district itself is on the National Register of Historic Places.

The theatre space within the old storefront is comfortable and charming, intimate and abuzz with energy; the company produces five to six shows each season in a space whose past life included being an entertainment venue for an eclectic array of performing arts. At one time, it was owned by the Costume Gallery located next door, considered one of Cincinnati's most outstanding costume shops.

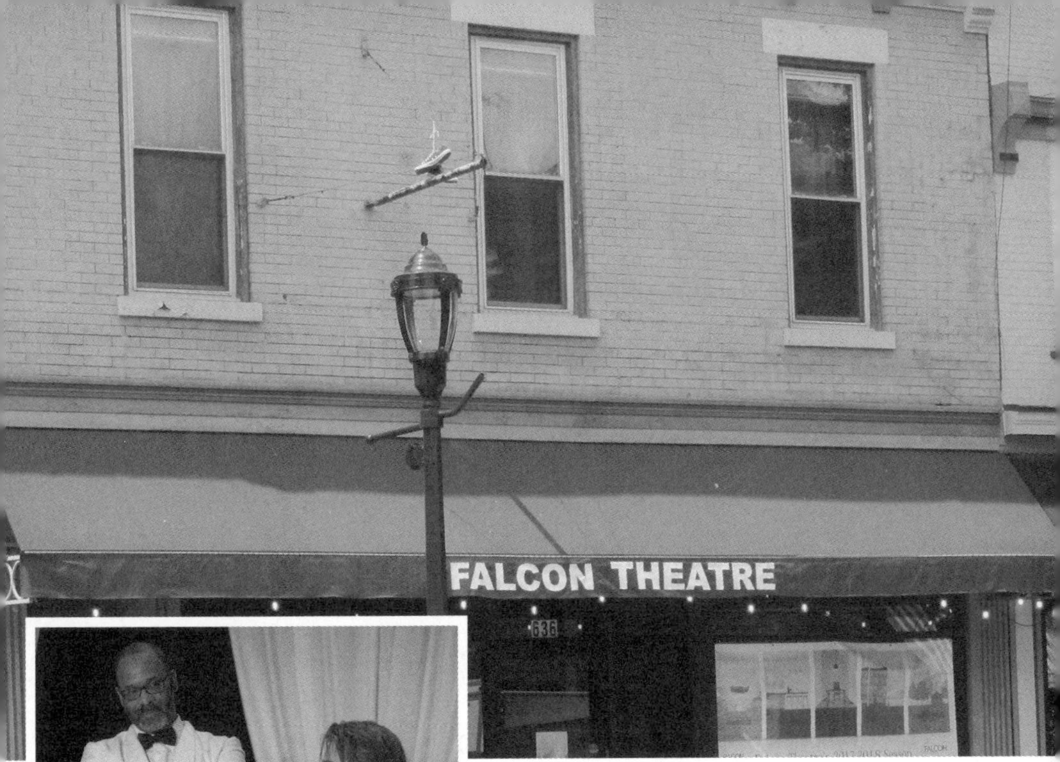

(Above) *The exceptional Falcon Theatre was founded by Dave Radtke and Ted Weil. Photo courtesy of John Witt.* (Left) *The Falcon Theatre staged "Master Harold" . . . And The Boys, a play that takes place in South Africa during the apartheid era, for its 2016-2017 season. Photo courtesy of Mikki Schaffner/ Used with permission by Falcon Theatre.*

Falcon Theatre moved lock, stock, and props into the space in 2004. The theatre purchased the building ten years later in 2014 and officially renamed it Falcon Theatre. And where does the Falcon Theatre company find many of the costumes for its productions? Right next door, of course, at the Costume Gallery.

---

Hope Juber, daughter of TV's iconic Sherwood Schwartz (*Gilligan's Island, The Brady Bunch*), wrote the songs for *Gilligan's Island: The Musical*, which is based on the 1960s TV series Schwartz created.

# 7 ALGIN OFFICE

## Why is a there a *Mad Men* vibe in a used office furniture store?

This office furniture store is so much more than office furniture, and that's the real secret to browsing this behemoth in downtown Cincinnati.

Seven humongous floors are packed with come-hithers, everything from a fabulous mix of used furniture running through the decades to a workshop inside the store where gorgeous made-to-order pieces are handcrafted from live edge slabs in a variety of species.

True, there are scads of used office desks and chairs and used hotel furnishings, but there is also a healthy dose of used Mid-Century Modern furniture, couches, china cabinets, dining room tables, and chairs and more that verily scream, *Mad Men*. Custom furniture is also here and next door at Algin Retro, which carries mostly Mid-Century Modern replicas and custom sofa and chair lines.

Algin's has been open for more than fifty years, although it used to be called Elgin's and sold guns and typewriters, practically the equivalent of a rock and chisel these days. It is a family business owned by Alan Weiss, whose grandfather originally opened the store.

Weiss brings an owner's enthusiasm to showing off what's to be found in this treasure chest, delighting in

### ALGIN OFFICE

**WHAT** Mid-Century Modern treasures

**WHERE** 810 Main St.

**COST** Free (and fun) to browse, but be forewarned— you will be tempted to buy.

**PRO TIP** The store is downtown, where free parking is always appreciated. Algin's validates at the All Pro Parking Lot at 830 Main St.

alginoffice.com

Algin Furniture
Office & Residential | EST. 1966
6 "The Attic"
Misc. Storage Warehouse
5 "Office World 2"
More Excellent Desks
& Used Office Chairs
4 "Office World"
Used Desks, Credenzas,
Conference Tables
3 "Slab City"
Live Edge Slabs
Urban Timber Workshop
2 "Ms. Cellaneous"
New & Used Residential
Bookcases & More!
1 "Show Room"
New Office Furniture
0 Basement
"Heavy Metal"
Metal Files & Cabinets
Algin Furniture
OFFICE and RESIDENTIAL
810 Main Street Cincinnati, OH | 513.621.1616 | AlginOffice.com

(Left) *Heywood-Wakefield dining set, including china cabinet, table and chairs, is a classic example of the midcentury modern design aesthetic.* (Right) *It's five floors of fabulous at Algin's. Photos courtesy of Algin Office.*

giving newbies and regulars alike an overview of what's where and what's recently arrived.

The journey begins when Weiss pulls the freight elevator doors together and you're transported up to the Attic. Work your way down to each successive floor by the back staircase: Office World and Office World 2; and Slab City, where master craftsmen in the Urban Timber Workshop create furniture from hunks of walnut, ash, maple, elm, pine, and even the more exotic monkeypod.

Ms. Cellaneous holds bookcases as well as new and used residential furniture, including cabinets, hutches, and other furnishings. The Showroom on the main floor displays new office furniture, along with a hodgepodge of used. Metal files and cabinets fill the basement, nicknamed Heavy Metal.

---

Algin's donates a portion of the proceeds from every Urban Timber sale to a local organization called Taking Root (www.takingroot.info), which plants new trees in the Greater Cincinnati area.

# 8 COOL GHOUL'S GRAVESITE

## In what cemetery can you find a real-life ghoul?

Blah, blah, blaaaaaaaaaaaaaah! If you grew up in Cincinnati in the 1970s, you immediately recognize this as the calling card of a certain Cool Ghoul.

Holding court over Saturday night TV for about three-and-a-half years, Richard "Dick" Von Hoene's onscreen horror host persona introduced *Scream-In*. The show premiered on WXIX-TV, Channel 19, a commercial channel that began broadcasting in August 1968, giving Cincinnati its fourth channel on the dial, a HUGE deal back then. The Cool Ghoul did the station proud.

Born in 1940 in Cincinnati's Price Hill neighborhood, Von Hoene also worked as a news anchor, television program host, and disc jockey. He was inducted into the Greater Cincinnati Legends of Rock 'n' Roll Hall of Fame in 1999.

*Scream-In* featured classic horror films from the 1940s through the 1960s with the Cool Ghoul camping it up with skits, bits, and jokes Von Hoene created and ad-libbed before, during, and after the movie. *The Angry Red Planet*, a 1959 sci-fi scarefest, was the first film screened on the program.

Horror genre gems like this one and others (1948's *Abbott & Costello Meet Frankenstein*, 1955's *It Came From Beneath the Sea*, and 1964's *Ghidrah, the Three-Headed Monster*), along with a lineup of guest stars, including another local fave, Larry Smith's *Hattie the Witch*, the Cool Ghoul's spot-on Boris Karloff

---

Boris Karloff, maestro of horror movies (*Frankenstein, The Mummy*), is beloved by children and adults alike for his non-horror dual role as Grinch and Narrator of the 1966 animated holiday classic, Dr. Seuss' *How the Grinch Stole Christmas.*

*Otherwise known as 19A, Lot 1, Grave 54, the Cool Ghoul's gravesite is located at Spring Grove Cemetery. Photo courtesy of John Witt.*

impressions, and sheer silliness, kept fans glued to their tiny television screens. Those lucky enough to have color TVs got full-on Cool Ghoul: screamingly bright orange-red fright wig, zany charcoaled eyes, trademark plaid hat.

Von Hoene died in 2004 at age sixty-three. Seven years later, in 2011, his Cool Ghoul was inducted into *Ripley's Believe It or Not Horror Host Hall of Fame*. He is buried at Spring Grove Cemetery where, according to Phil Nuxhall's *Stories in the Grove*, a pumpkin is placed at his gravestone every Halloween.

## COOL GHOUL'S GRAVESITE

**WHAT** Cemetery spirit

**WHERE** Spring Grove Cemetery & Arboretum, 4521 Spring Grove Ave.

**COST** Free.

**PRO TIP** For such a big personality, Von Hoene's tombstone is fairly modest, inscribed with the sentiment, "Always in our hearts."

springgrove.org

# 9 DINSMORE HOMESTEAD

**Where can you snoop into a lady's personal papers without reprimand?**

*". . . I drudge and worry to no avail, lose money & temper and hope, I feel so unlike a lady in my external that I have no doubt I shall soon be less a lady in reality, associating only with coarse people all against me in their own interest, and never having one day of leisure or pleasure in which I can be my own old self again, Lord send me a fool who wants to pay a good price for this place."*

Julia Stockton Dinsmore wrote these words on January 21, 1875, three years after losing her father, the last member of her immediate family. Amazingly, she kept journals for fifty-four years, recording everything from the prosaic to the profound.

Visitors to the Dinsmore Homestead, a Cincinnati treasure that narrates the life and times of the Dinsmores, a rural family that farmed the land through generations, can read this journal entry and others, while experiencing a house

## DINSMORE HOMESTEAD

**WHAT** Nineteenth-century homestead

**WHERE** 5656 Burlington Pike, Burlington, KY

**COST** $7 adults; $3 ages five-fifteen; free under five.

**PRO TIP** Tours are given Fridays, Saturdays, and Sundays, beginning on the hour, 1–5 p.m., April 1–December 15. Events take place throughout the year.

dinsmorefarm.org

Dinsmore visitors love learning about mourning traditions, like cutting hair from the dead or dying and saving it in rings or brooches. Julia Dinsmore remembered friends' and relatives' "death day" as well as their birthday.

(Above) *At the Dinsmore Homestead, nearly all the accumulated contents of the home and outbuildings still survive.* (Right) *The smokehouse at the Dinsmore Homestead. Photos courtesy of John Witt.*

that looks as though the occupants simply got up and wandered off.

That's because every single item in the house (excluding the silver on the dining room table), from a handmade doll with nut head to a circa 1842 bed from McAlpin's to a mort cloth, which was laid on coffins when mourners came to pay their respects, is original to the home. This includes ninety thousand pages of family documents (Julia's journals among them) and receipts for furniture visitors see.

"James Dinsmore's great-great-granddaughter, Martha Breasted, who visited here in the 1970s and 1980s, wanted visitors to feel like they were walking into a living house where the owner had just stepped out to call on a neighbor," said Cathy Collopy, education coordinator.

The family owned the house until 1987; the Dinsmore Homestead Foundation purchased it in 1988 and operates it today.

# 10 CAPITOLINE SHE-WOLF STATUE

## Why did an Italian dictator gift Cincinnati with a statue based on a symbol from Roman mythology?

What a statue it is! The Capitoline She-Wolf Statue. Poised on a marble pedestal in a serene and shaded area at Eden Park's Twin Lakes overlook is a bronze she-wolf with thick neck and benign expression suckling two babies. And they're not mere ordinary babies, but Romulus and Remus, of founders of Rome fame, according to mythology, the very twin babies abandoned as infants on the banks of the Tiber River and saved by the she-wolf.

The original, an ancient Etruscan statue that dates back to the Middle Ages, is in Rome's Capitoline Museums, which explains the name. Cincinnati's statue is of a more recent vintage. It was gifted to the city in 1932 by the City of Rome through an arrangement by the Sons of Italy and courtesy of Italian dictator Benito Mussolini. The creator of the Fascist Party, executed in 1945, wanted to mark the tenth year of his regime.

Mussolini sent replica statues to a number of other cities in the United States, including Rome, Georgia, and Rome, New York, and it's easy to see the connection. But Cincinnati?

Apparently, Mussolini chose the Queen City because it was named after Cincinnatus (519–430 BC), the Roman statesman

---

Don't look for a mention of Mussolini. (There isn't one.) *Il governatore di Roma alla citta Cincinnati* is etched into the statue's base, and a nearby plaque narrates the story of Remus and Romulus.

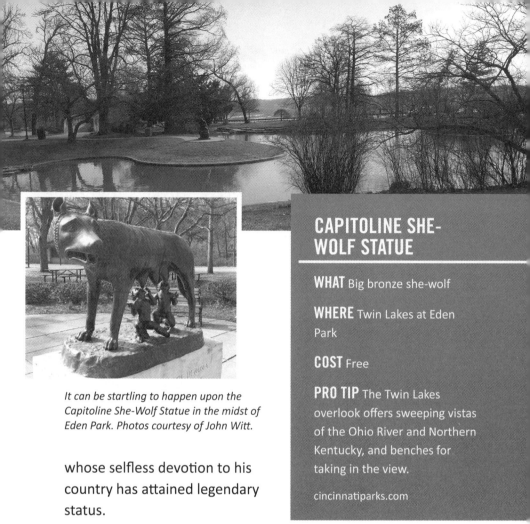

*It can be startling to happen upon the Capitoline She-Wolf Statue in the midst of Eden Park. Photos courtesy of John Witt.*

## CAPITOLINE SHE-WOLF STATUE

**WHAT** Big bronze she-wolf

**WHERE** Twin Lakes at Eden Park

**COST** Free

**PRO TIP** The Twin Lakes overlook offers sweeping vistas of the Ohio River and Northern Kentucky, and benches for taking in the view.

cincinnatiparks.com

whose selfless devotion to his country has attained legendary status.

But the joke is on Mussolini, because Cincinnati isn't named for Cincinnatus *exactly*, but for the Order of the Cincinnatus (sometimes called the Society of the Cincinnati), which was formed by a group of former Revolutionary War officers who wanted to recall the Roman legend. None other than George Washington was its first president.

Louis Leonard Tucker lays it out in *Cincinnati's Citizen Crusaders: A History of The Cincinnatus Association 1920–1965*. (The organization derives its name from those same roots.) Arthur St. Clair, a member of the Order of Cincinnatus and Governor-General of the Northwest Territory, applied the name in 1790.

Take that, Il Duce.

# 11 EARLY SCHOOLHOUSE

## Why is an old log cabin sitting in a concrete complex?

From a rustic and barebones one-room schoolhouse to a thoroughly modern university with such high-tech teaching tools as a Center for Applied Informatics and Digitorium with amped-up digital media wall and viewing opera boxes, the road to a good education has certainly changed over time.

Case in point: A log cabin looking straight out of *Little House on the Prairie* squats at the entrance to the campus of Northern Kentucky University (NKU), seeming a bit lost amidst a concrete city of state-of-the-art, architecturally arresting buildings, all teched out to the hilt. Still, this book-learning forebear has a lot to teach about education, from its humble beginnings to a legacy of dedication to scholarship.

Built circa 1849 in Grants Lick, Kentucky, the cabin was sold at some point and took up residence in Alexandria, Kentucky. From here, it went to A.J. Jolly Park in the mid-1970s (possibly around the time of the US Bicentennial celebration in 1976) and then onward in the early 1980s to the campus at NKU.

### EARLY SCHOOLHOUSE

**WHAT** Log cabin school

**WHERE** Northern Kentucky University, Nunn Dr., Highland Heights, KY

**COST** Free

**PRO TIP** The cabin is not currently open to the public, but visitors are free to tour the grounds and visit the garden.

nku.edu

---

In spring 2017, the NKU Wildflower Garden was added to the grounds behind the Early Schoolhouse to showcase plants native to Kentucky's landscape before it was settled.

(Above) *The Early Schoolhouse perches atop a hill near the entrance to the Northern Kentucky University campus.* (Left) *The NKU Wildflower Garden is planted behind the Early Schoolhouse. Photos courtesy of John Witt.*

Local lore suggests the cabin was actually part of a home that was used as a school for the children of the local community, who would most likely have been taught by one of their neighbors.

Renovations made over time include the removal of cement chinking and chicken wire and the addition of framing to the windows and door. Plans are in the works to restore and furnish the interior, with an eye toward eventually using the cabin as an outdoor laboratory.

Those pioneer-students of long ago would surely be pleased to see the place where they learned their three Rs (reading, 'riting, and 'rithmetic) still in use as a community gathering place and center of learning.

# 12 BOBBY MACKEY'S MUSIC WORLD

### What makes this place the most haunted nightclub in America?

Actually, the more accurate question is who. Zak Bagans, American paranormal investigator and host of the Travel Channel series *Ghost Adventures*, declared this former slaughterhouse and meatpacking operation turned hopping honky-tonk to be the "Most Haunted Nightclub in America."

Bagans and his TV film crew came to Bobby Mackey's Music World in 2008 to investigate claims of rampant paranormal activity and found what other visitors have experienced (being touched by a presence, seeing shadow figures, hearing disembodied voices) to be true. In fact, hundreds of people, both those who have taken the club's haunted tour and patrons of the bar on weekends, have experienced the ghostly phenomena.

If you think all the stuff taking place on the inside of this Wilder, Kentucky, bar is scary, wait until you pull up and see the outside. It is a whipstitch assemblage of dilapidated structures with sagging roofline that pretty much screams, "paranormal activity

#### BOBBY MACKEY'S MUSIC WORLD

**WHAT** Haunted honky-tonk

**WHERE** 44 Licking Pike, Wilder, KY

**COST** Tours are $35 per person ($25 per person, four or more) or, for those stout-hearted souls who would like to conduct their own investigation, a five-hour private and unguided experience is $595 for up to twelve. Request a tour at gatekeeperparanormal.com/book-a-tour

**PRO TIP** Both the two-hour and the five-hour tours start at 7, 8, or 9 p.m.

bobbymackey.com

*Country music and ghosts share the space at Bobby Mackey's Music World. Photo courtesy of John Witt.*

takes place here!" Still, when weekends roll around, it rocks with country music entertainment, karaoke, and line dancing.

Sunday through Thursday evenings are set aside for two-hour guided tours into the paranormal realm. The rough-and-tumble tavern has a long and storied history that involves murders, gangsters, jilted lovers, even a demonic possession. Afternoon tours are also offered Monday through Thursday between late August and May and year-round on Sundays.

Some of it is the stuff of legends; much of it is fact. As you travel through each of the building's three floors, including the basement, the tour guide (a member of Bobby Mackey's Official Paranormal Team) will separate fact from fiction and discuss reported paranormal activity.

Plenty of time is allotted to investigate and search for evidence of the paranormal. Ghost hunters should bring a camera, recorder, EMF (electromagnetic field) meter, and any other small, handheld equipment needed.

---

Ghost hunters are free to investigate on their own at a five-hour investigation. Bring video cameras and DVR systems. An Official Paranormal Team guide will remain in the building (and help bolster your courage).

# 13 CHILDREN'S THEATRE OF CINCINNATI

## How does such a well-known venue keep such a big secret?

The Children's Theatre of Cincinnati has a thoroughly smitten fanbase. After all, the theatre has been around for more than ninety seasons, and those-in-the-know don't waste time snapping up tickets.

What is not-so-well-known is the absolute top-rate quality of each and every production staged.

Way back in 1924, at the height of the Jazz Age, the Junior League of Cincinnati created the Junior League Players to bring theatre to Cincinnati's young and young-at-heart. Two years after the end of World War II, the Children's Theatre was incorporated and set out to become a force among professional theatre companies. It succeeded.

While patrons are routinely blown away by enchanted carriages sweeping onto the stage, quick-change costume wizardry right before their eyes, and characters flying off into the nether regions, those who have never had the pleasure of witnessing a show are missing out on some of the best theatre in town, and that is saying something in an exceptional theatre town like Cincinnati.

Here is theatre *for* kids, not *by* kids, an important distinction and one that has set a standard for professional-level quality

---

The Taft Theatre is a Neo-Classical/Art Deco treasure built in 1928 and renovated several years ago to bring it into the twenty-first century while retaining its historic character and ambience.

*Cast members from The Children's Theatre's world-premiere production of "Alice in Wonderland" take the stage. Photo courtesy of Mikki Schaffner/Courtesy of The Children's Theatre of Cincinnati.*

## THE CHILDREN'S THEATRE OF CINCINNATI

**WHAT** Outstanding theatre for kids

**WHERE** Fifth & Sycamore Sts.

**COST** Single ticket prices vary.

**PRO TIP** There is patron drop-off/pick-up directly in front of the Taft Theatre. Parking lots and garages are within two to three blocks.

thechildrenstheatre.com

seen in every aspect of each show, from an extraordinary caliber of talent among the actors, singers, and dancers to sets that never fail to mesmerize to costuming tailor-made for whatever zany cast of characters is taking the stage.

Productions are junior versions of beloved classics like *Peter Pan, The Wizard of Oz, Mary Poppins, Charlotte's Web, The Jungle Book*, and more. Characters are favorite childhood friends: Charlie Brown, Shrek, Annie, Elf, Willy Wonka, Jack (of beanstalk fame), Rudolph the Red-Nosed Reindeer, and others.

Performances take place within the grand and historic 2,500-seat Taft Theatre. Seats are comfy, and views are unobstructed, which is good, because you won't want to miss a single second of what's unfolding on stage.

# 14 GLENWOOD GARDENS

## What Cincinnati park is like an adventure in Alice's wonderland?

Hidden in plain view within a suburban landscape leaning toward industrial is a true Cincinnati gem: The 335-acre Glenwood Gardens is a land of enchantment with formal gardens, forests, wetlands and prairies, and the twelve-acre Highfield Discovery Garden, which looks straight out of a mashed-up fairy tale.

Floating bees in the Cotswold Visitor Center. A twenty-five-foot Discovery Tree, its mouth gaping wide to swallow up little hide-and-seekers. Choo choo trains chugging through Trolley Garden. Colorful, ginormous mushrooms and other whimsies. Here is a children's storybook come to life.

Seven different gardens cast a spell, from the Wizard's Garden, with its bouncy bridge, to Grandma's Scent Garden and its kid-sized cottage set for a tea party to the Butterfly Garden, which is shaped like its star resident. Dig in dirt, pump water, cross a frog pond, romp through a spiraling caterpillar tunnel. Beware the dragon standing watch at the Fairy Garden.

Kids can stage a puppet show, play at interactive computer game stations, listen in to storytime, and participate in hands-on classes and events: container gardening, fairies, nighttime hiking, concerts, and art fairs. A bridge ushers visitors into the quieter world of the Wetland Loop.

---

Purchase an annual family pass to the Highfield Discovery Garden. For $45 for a family of four, you could visit every day the park is open plus get perks like discounts in the gift shop.

*See demonstration gardens along the Garden Loop and different habitats along the Wetland Loop at Glenwood Gardens. Photo courtesy of John Witt.*

## GLENWOOD GARDENS

**WHAT** Storybook gardens

**WHERE** 10397 Springfield Pike, Woodlawn, OH

**COST** An annual Motor Vehicle Permit is required: $10/ Hamilton County residents; $14/all others.

**PRO TIP** Register for classes and programs early. Spots tend to fill up fast for gardening classes, yearly programs, and evening events.

greatparks.org

The Highfield Discovery Garden is unique among the region's parks, as is Glenwood itself. It is the only park in the Great Parks system with gardens as its main feature. The one-mile garden loop beyond the overlook is an easy stroll to see more than a dozen species of native trees and a sea of wildflowers, a charming bridge trimmed in black railing, and architectural ornaments salvaged from the circa 1880s Chamber of Commerce building.

Also tucked away in the garden is a burial mound believed to have been built by either the Adena or Hopewell Indians of the Woodland era. Dating back to 500 B.C. to 350 A.D., it is on the National Register of Historic Places.

# 15 AMERICAN SIGN MUSEUM

**Why is one of the most ubiquitous and seen products in the world an almost completely invisible industry?**

You see hundreds of them wherever you are and wherever you go. Every. Single. Day. There's no escaping them or their messages: "Ohio Welcomes You." "Ice." "Beer." "Hamburgers." "Hotel." "Danger."

Signs.

They are everywhere, enticing, directing, and warning us. Yet they sort of fade into the surrounding landscape. The repository for the industry's signage is a little-known gem located in Cincinnati that is actually the largest public sign museum in the country: the American Sign Museum.

To step into this colorful and sometimes manic world of messaging is to be blown away by the sheer size and scope of the signage within. From pre-electric signs to modern plastic signs and every manufacturing material and method in between, the museum covers more than one hundred years of American sign history along a tech and design timeline that meanders over twenty thousand square feet.

See Main Street Any Town USA with its explosion of signage alerting shoppers to hardware, appliances, radios and TVs, drugs, pizza, a barber shop, Mexican food, and more. Read a Burma Shave sign sequence: "Their product good/but ours/does what/you think it should." Visit a room packed with

---

Burma-Shave (brushless shaving cream) was famous for posting a succession of signs along the highway. The rhyming poems unspooled verse by verse along the sequence, ending with punchline and product name.

*Learn the stories behind a century of signs at the American Sign Museum. Photo courtesy of John Witt.*

local vintage Cincinnati signs for Suders Art Store, Budna Grill, Wizard Records, and Kroger. Wander among salesman's samples, neons, flashers, clocks, thermometers, even a rotating Big Boy.

The signs come from all over the United States, represent every decade going back a century, and give clues not only about their place in history, but America's, too, based on their design, materials, color scheme, and typeface.

## AMERICAN SIGN MUSEUM

**WHAT** Sign, sign, everywhere a sign

**WHERE** 1330 Monmouth Ave.

**COST** $15 adults; $10 seniors, students, military; three children (twelve and under) are free with each paid admission (tickets may be purchased online at americansignmuseum.org).

**PRO TIP** Weekday public tours include a demo from NeonWorks of Cincinnati, located within the museum.

# 16 HAIL DARK AESTHETICS

## Where can you find discount animal skulls, witchy whatnots, and Elvis albums under one roof?

They're creepy and they're kooky/mysterious and spooky/ They're altogether ooky . . . and we're not talking about the 1960s TV series, although Morticia and Gomez and the rest of the Adamms Family would be perfectly at home in the eerie ambiance of Hail Dark Aesthetics.

The shop is a cabinet of curiosities spilling over with oddities and novelties: a two-headed calf; stuffed dead animal heads; a head shot of one of the most famous prom queens of all times, Laura Palmer from the 1990s cult TV series *Twin Peaks* (and no, things didn't end well for her); mummified cats; handmade and possibly enchanted jewelry; and Baphomet flags plastered with the image of the mystical deity.

You'll find all these wonders and more, along with crystal balls, medical equipment that will send chills down your spine, animal skulls, vintage religious iconography, and Ouija boards, tarot cards, and other portals to the dark arts arrayed on the shelves or mounted on the walls at one of the coolest shops in Covington's MainStrasse Village, and in the Cincinnati area in general.

Book titles indicate that shopkeeps Neil and J. D. get their audience: *Satan Speaks, Lords of Chaos*, and *The Seven Addictions and Five Professions of Anita Berber: Weimar*

---

The shop has a killer inventory of vinyl: rock, pop, hip-hop, folk, R&B, classical, and more. If you're looking to augment your album collection, spend a fun hour or so flipping through the stacks here.

*Inventory changes frequently at Hail Dark Aesthetics, but it is always spectacularly weird and decidedly dark. Photo courtesy of John Witt.*

*Berlin's Priestess of Depravity*, the first contemporary biography of the notorious dancer, actress, and star of the 1921 silent epic *Lucifer*, whose vast sexual harem counted Marlene Dietrich and the King of Yugoslavia among its members.

For weird, dark, and creepy, this is the place. The staff is easy to talk to and very helpful. How could you be otherwise in a shop that nosedived straight into the macabre?

## HAIL DARK AESTHETICS

**WHAT** Oddities and albums

**WHERE** 720 Main St., Covington, KY

**COST** Free to browse, but you'll probably find something you can't live without. Prices range from a few dollars on up.

**PRO TIP** You may be greeted by a taxidermy goat with a book open in its lap, but this shop is pure ghoulish good fun.

hailcincinnati.com

# 17 BEHRINGER-CRAWFORD MUSEUM

## What do a two-headed calf and shrunken head have to do with area regional history?

That beautiful building perched on a hilltop that looks like someone's personal residence is in fact a priceless repository for artifacts and information relating to the history of Northern Kentucky's people and past.

Rising on a gentle slope in Covington's beautiful Devou Park is the Behringer-Crawford Museum, formerly the home of the Devou family, who owned it from the 1880s to 1910, when they donated it to the City of Covington to be used as a park. It is named for world-traveling eccentric William Behringer, whose collection of "curiosities" was the genesis of the museum, and archaeologist Ellis Crawford, the museum's first curator.

Its early days were devoted to displaying Behringer's oddities: a life-sized stuffed black bear, American Indian artifacts, the two-headed calf, and the shrunken head, all of which may still be seen. Over the years, the museum has expanded with additional displays and exhibits.

Find the 1892 streetcar named *Kentucky*, parked in the museum's lobby; a giant paddlewheel steamboat, a

### BEHRINGER-CRAWFORD MUSEUM

**WHAT** A shrunken head and expanded exhibits

**WHERE** 1600 Montague Rd., Covington, KY

**COST** $9 adults; $8 seniors; $5 children ages three to seventeen (tickets may be purchased online at bcmuseum.org). Parking is free.

**PRO TIP** Visit during the holidays to see the outstanding Holiday Toy Trains: Two hundred fifty-plus feet of model train tracks and lots of buttons to push.

(Above) *The museum offers a comprehensive portrait of Northern Kentucky, its people, its history, and evolution from prehistoric times to the present, its arts and culture, its spirit.* (Left) *Visiting the holiday trains, Charles Dickens display and more at Behringer-Crawford Museum is a Cincinnati tradition. Photos courtesy of Behringer-Crawford Museum.*

salute to Ohio River history; a train enthusiast's idealized re-creation of a mid-century community in miniature that comes to life with working trains, lights, and voices and has a kid-sized tunnel to unique viewing bubbles; and exhibits that cover industry, art, politics, frontier life, the Civil War, and more.

You can "fish" from the side of the *Wake Robin*, an interactive learning center; have a tea party; slide into a vintage Buick Electra for a drive-in experience to watch old newsreels; bebop to the tunes playing on the jukebox; see memorabilia relating to the legendary paddle wheeler, the *Delta Queen*, and so much more. The museum is a charming place to while away an afternoon, with or without kids.

---

Listen carefully. Do you hear footsteps? The museum may be haunted, but don't worry. These ghosts, allegedly seen in the galleries and looking out windows (and heard in the vacant upper floors), are benevolent.

# 18 FLEISCHMANN GARDENS

**How did a good loaf of bread lead to one of Cincinnati's loveliest parks?**

Enter through the beautiful ornamental iron gates crowned by an old-fashioned gaslight fixture and stroll into the hush of Fleischmann Gardens, a trim and tidy four-acre garden respite in Cincinnati's Avondale neighborhood.

The park was a gift to the city, presented nearly a century ago in 1925 by the heirs of Charles Fleischmann, the founder of the Fleischmann Yeast Company and reason Americans can enjoy light and delicious loaves of bread.

## FLEISCHMANN GARDENS

**WHAT** Garden mazes

**WHERE** 524 Forest Ave.

**COST** Free

**PRO TIP** The park's scenic iron gate entrance is located on Washington Ave. in Avondale.

cincinnatiparks.com

Originally from Budapest, Hungary, Fleischmann and his brother Maximilian came to the United States in the 1860s and, in short order, revolutionized home and commercial baking in 1868 with the invention of a patented compressed yeast cake. Less than a decade later, they had achieved household-name status. The innovations continued with Active Dry Yeast created in the World War II years; RapidRise Yeast, innovated in 1984; and bread-machine yeast landing on the table in 1993.

But back to the gardens. Part of the Cincinnati Parks system, the gardens are immaculately groomed and flourish on the site that was formerly the Fleishmann family home. A stone path leads to steps that descend to four precision-planted and perfectly symmetrical evergreen garden mazes.

(Above) *Fleischmann Gardens is a pint-size paradise in Avondale.* (Left) *A portion of Fleischmann Gardens is devoted to a maze garden. Photos courtesy of John Witt.*

Within the gardens' black fencing are flower beds, a raised plaza, an arbor, and a six-foot boulder marking the site of the Fleishmann home. A children's playground offers a climbing structure and swing set. Rising majestically above all is the largest ginkgo tree in the state of Ohio.

---

At age twenty-eight, Charles's son, Julius Augustus Fleischmann (1871–1925), became Cincinnati's youngest mayor in 1900. At that point, the sailor, sportsman, and businessman had already been the president of the Fleischmann Yeast Company for three years.

# 19 ARNOLD'S BAR & GRILL

## How did the oldest bar in Cincinnati become the canvas for three of the world's greatest street artists?

For the historic and humble Arnold's Bar & Grill, a downtown Cincinnati icon that has operated as a bar since 1861, hosting the hottest street artists was as easy as offering up a wall.

Activist/illustrator/street artist Shepard Fairey; self-described *photograffeur* JR; and Hargo, whose famous *Cash for Your Warhol* still has people calling the phone number on this plaque, are considered to be among the most important street artists of the twenty-first century. During individual visits to town, each left his unique and decidedly contemporary imprint on walls of the structure (actually two buildings) originally built in the late 1830s.

The murals add a distinctive if underappreciated flourish to an establishment that determinedly maintains its diamond-in-the-rough atmosphere and appearance, so customers feel like they're walking into an old-time saloon. Think worn and creaky floors, wopperjawed staircases, and a second-floor bathtub that dates to the Prohibition era, when then-owner Hugo Arnold would whip up homemade spirits.

"People pass these murals every day without realizing just how big a deal they are," said manager Chris Breeden.

For those who do tune in, they will discover that art is everywhere their eyes travel within Arnold's, too, including

---

Catch Arnold's annual holiday show. It is a little naughty, a lot nice and funny, and is typically produced by Cincinnati's Know Theatre and OTRImprov. Performances take place on the courtyard stage.

## ARNOLD'S BAR & GRILL

**WHAT** Street art meets pub grub

**WHERE** 210 E. Eighth St.

**COST** Dinner entrées under $20 per person (see menu at arnoldsbarandgrill.com).

**PRO TIP** No need to buy anything to enjoy the Shepard Fairey and Hargo (aka Cash For Your Warhol) murals at Arnold's. They are located on the restaurant's exterior alley wall.

*Look closely and you will spot renowned street artist Shepard Fairey's artwork gracing the building of Arnold's Bar & Grill. Photo courtesy of Alias Imaging/Arnold's.*

stained glass, a neon sign,and several autographed cast photos from the Kathy Bates TV drama, *Harry's Law*, which was set in Cincinnati. In search of authenticity, the show's producers visited and then built an Arnold's set in Hollywood as the watering hole where the legal misfits hang out.

The artwork is a bonus to the restaurant's outstanding comfort cuisine menu, which keeps things perennially interesting by changing often; impressive draft and bourbon lists as well as on-trend cocktails; enchanting enclosed courtyard seating; and nightly live local music, which tends toward Americana, blues, and jazz performed on the stage in the courtyard.

# 20 ELSINORE ARCH

## If "all the world's a stage," how did it wind up in Cincinnati?

For at least a few generations of Cincinnatians, Elsinore Arch (also known as Elsinore Tower) is inextricably intertwined with memories of the Cincinnati Museum of Natural History and Planetarium's 1957-constructed building and childhood visits that included spine-tingling strolls across the glass-floored bridges in the museum's darkened cave.

Located on Gilbert Avenue at Elsinore Place, this castlesque structure was actually built as a valve station to control water flow from the Eden Park reservoir. Inspiration for the design, incredibly enough, came from a stage set of a local production of *Hamlet* in 1883, the year Cincinnati hosted the Shakespearean Dramatic Festival at Music Hall.

The enormous set painting depicted Denmark's Kronborg Castle, aka Elsinore Castle, the very castle in which Shakespeare set Hamlet back in the 1600s. Cincinnati Water Works Superintendent A.G. Moore saw the play, and the painting, and was smitten.

At the time, Cincinnati Water Works was planning to extend its water supply main tunnel from Eden Park to Gilbert Avenue. Aesthetics was critical. All involved wanted something that would not only enhance the landscape but also act as an entry to the park.

---

In 1990, the Cincinnati Museum of Natural History became the Museum of Natural History & Science and took up residence inside the multi-museum complex, Cincinnati Museum Center at Union Terminal.

## ELSINORE ARCH

**WHAT** Hamlet's castle

**WHERE** 1292–1298 Elsinore Ave.

**COST** Free

**PRO TIP** WCPO-TV Studio sits in place of the old museum and planetarium and was constructed with stonework similar to that used in the arch's construction.

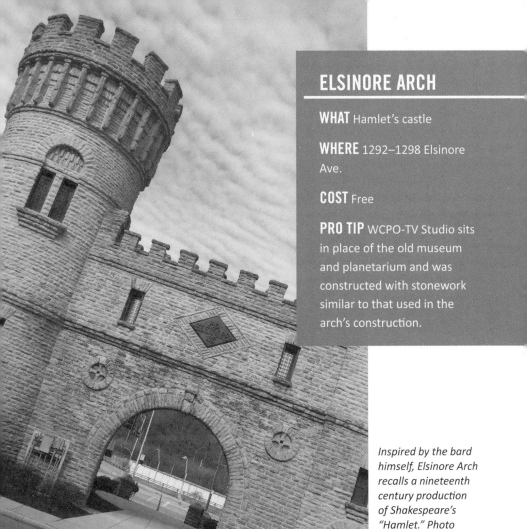

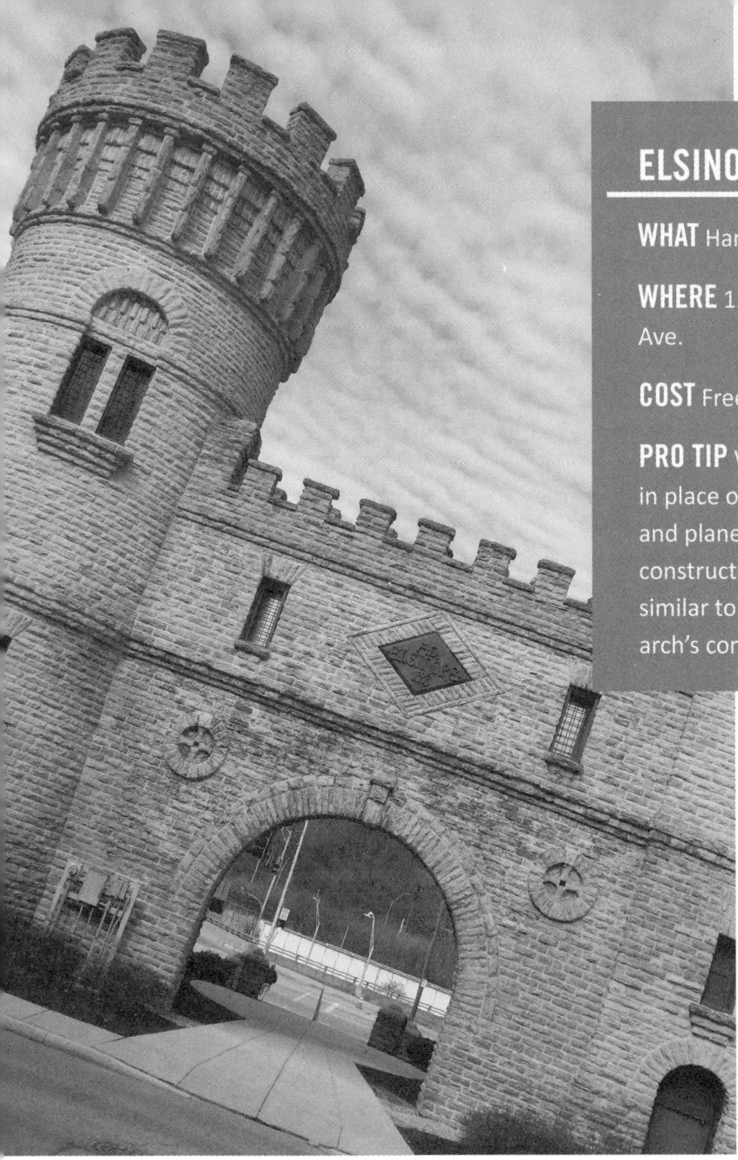

*Inspired by the bard himself, Elsinore Arch recalls a nineteenth century production of Shakespeare's "Hamlet." Photo courtesy of John Witt.*

One visit to famous Cincinnati architect Samuel Hannaford (who also built the Cincinnati Observatory's 1873 building) later and it was decided: The valve house would be Elsinore Castle in miniature, its Norman Romanesque Revival style mimicking aspects of Kronborg, including a circular castellated tower and a smaller square. Connecting the two: a battlemented archway. Completed later in 1883, the arch is listed on the National Register of Historic Places.

# 21 FUTURO HOUSE

## How did a space ship land in a residential neighborhood?

The design was lightyears ahead of its time, looking more like something found on a Hollywood backlot for a low-budget B movie than tucked into a residential neighborhood not far from the Ohio River: Futuro House. More UFO than humble abode with its circular shape and porthole-like windows, this Covington house at one time reflected the new frontier of housing.

Designed by Finnish architect Matti Suuronen, Futuro House was a lightweight prefab made of fiberglass-reinforced plastic, fully assembled and designed to be dropped into any climate and topography. Suuronen came up with the idea in 1968, a time when the world was caught in the throes of the Space Race and the United States was a year and one giant leap away from landing the first man on the moon on July 16, 1969.

Suuronen's original intent was for his Space Age structure to serve as a portable ski chalet or holiday home. The European models offered three hundred square feet; the ones for the United States were a more bloated five hundred or so. A retractable hatch stairway, just like a "real" flying saucer, provided entry.

Floorplans featured living and dining areas, kitchen, bath, and bedroom with double bed-seat (plus an additional six bed seats located in the house) centered around a fireplace/

---

On November 2, 2013, Futuro House Day in Covington, then-mayor Sherry Carran made an official proclamation, unofficially dubbing the area surrounding Futuro House "Area 89," a tie-in to local ClassX radio station 89.1 FM.

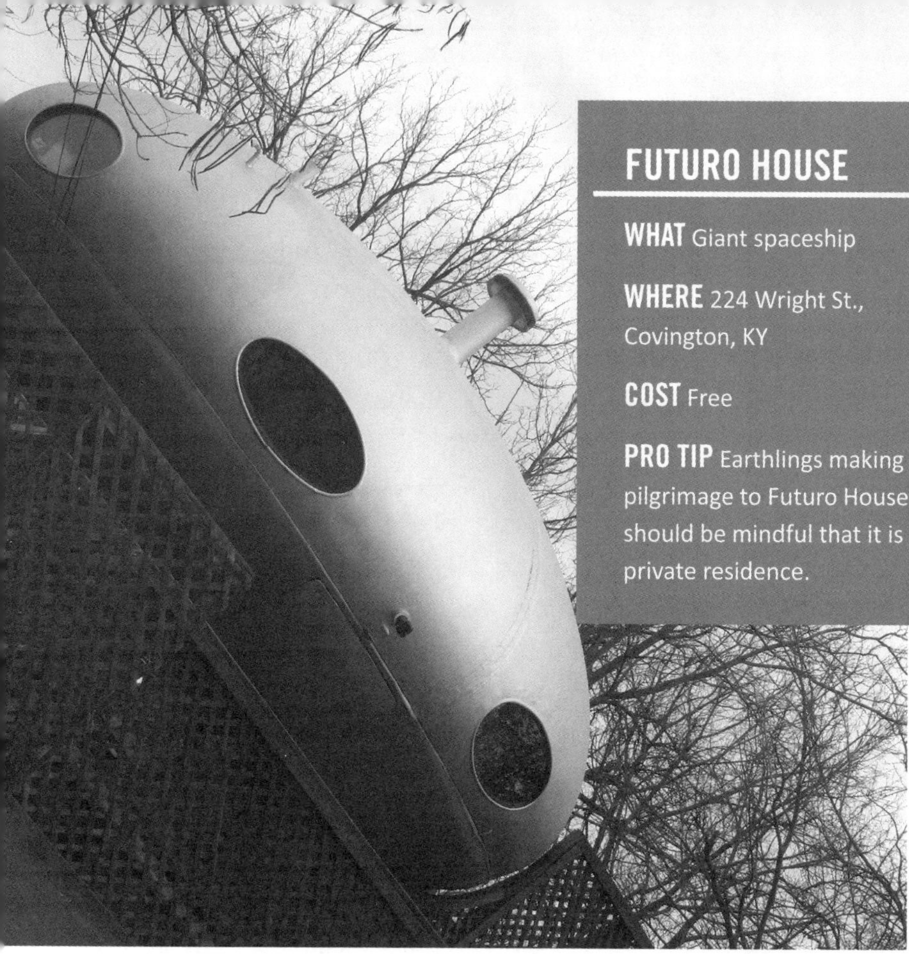

## FUTURO HOUSE

**WHAT** Giant spaceship

**WHERE** 224 Wright St., Covington, KY

**COST** Free

**PRO TIP** Earthlings making the pilgrimage to Futuro House should be mindful that it is a private residence.

*It's back to the future with Futuro House. Photo courtesy of John Witt.*

barbecue grill with space to slide a stereo beneath. The original open concept. Furnishings were custom designed.

Less than one hundred Futuro Houses were made (owing in part to the oil crisis in 1973). The remaining handful are sprinkled around the globe, including in Covington. Visible from the Brent Spence Bridge, this alien spacecraft perched amidst craftsman-style homes was purchased by Rob Wetzel in 1976 and installed on this no-outlet street in the mid-1980s. A number of ensuing renovations (a second hatch, more windows, heated cabana bar addition) have made this Futuro House unique, even among its own kind.

# 22 HAVEN GILLESPIE HOUSE

**How is one of the most beloved seasonal standards tied to Cincinnati?**

You better watch out. You better not cry. And you better know the rest of the words to one of the most popular and enduring Christmas songs ever penned, "Santa Claus Is Coming to Town."

The song was written by James "Haven" Lamont Gillespie in 1933 (with composer J. Fred Coots). Scribbled down during a New York subway ride, it would earn millions for the lyricist whose family had once been so poor they lived in the basement of a Third Street home in Covington.

Gillespie was born here on February 6, 1888, and lived in various homes in the area off and on until 1950, when he moved to Hollywood. He also worked here, including stints as a typesetter at the *Cincinnati Enquirer* and *Cincinnati Times-Star*. One of the homes was 509 Montgomery Street, built in 1909. Gillespie lived in this home with his wife, Corene, through the 1930s and 1940s.

This house is one of the few area touchstones for this Christmas song chartbuster. At one point, he was remembered along with area notables with a historical marker at Goebel Park in MainStrasse. In 2014, however, the marker was deemed damaged beyond repair and removed.

### HAVEN GILLESPIE HOUSE

**WHAT** Holiday classic composer

**WHERE** 509 Montgomery St., Covington, KY

**COST** Free

**PRO TIP** In the Covington City Directories of the 1930s and 1940s, Haven Gillespie is listed as a freelance songwriter living at 509 Montgomery St. in Covington.

*Haven Gillespie was inducted into the Songwriters Hall of Fame in 1970. He died on March 14, 1975, in Las Vegas. Photo courtesy of John Witt.*

Gillespie started writing songs in 1911 and is considered among the best of the Tin Pan Alley songwriters of the 1930s and 1940s. Among his more than one thousand original compositions are such classic hits as "You Go To My Head," "By the Sycamore Tree," and the Christmas song that became an overnight sensation as soon as it was performed on Eddie Cantor's radio show in 1934.

"Santa Claus Is Coming to Town" has been recorded by dozens of artists, including Tommy Dorsey & His Orchestra, Perry Como, Gene Autry, the Four Seasons, the Jackson Five, Bruce Springsteen and the E Street Band, and Mariah Carey.

---

The 1970 animated film, *Santa Claus Is Coming to Town*, voiced by famous Hollywood hoofer Fred Astaire and *Andy Hardy* star Mickey Rooney, was based on Gillespie's classic song.

# 23 FERNALD PRESERVE

## Why are bobolinks, grasshopper sparrows, and the rarely spotted Eurasian Wigeon making themselves at home at a once-contaminated nuclear weapons plant?

Walk the site that was once a uranium processing facility and, since 2006, the pride of several government and community agencies that collaborated to create a celebrated 1,050-acre wetlands and prairie.

Owned by the US Department of Energy and overseen by its Office of Legacy Management, the Fernald Preserve stretches across the site of the former Cold War–era Feed Materials Production Center. Here, high-purity uranium metal products—in other words, materials for nuclear bombs—were produced from 1951 to 1989. Since Fernald's massive environmental and ecological restoration, 245 species of birds have been observed on this reclaimed land.

Where factories and warehouses once stood are now 140 acres of wetland habitats, one of the largest manmade wetlands in Ohio, which shelter and nurture a diverse wildlife population. There are three lakes; more than 350 acres of grasslands, including tall-grass prairies; and 400 acres of forests. Visitors can stroll along a seven-mile trail system to see the various habitats and perhaps catch sight of (and a photograph) their occupants.

---

The trails at this regionally recognized birding hotspot showcase different scenes within the preserve. The Lodge Pond Trail meanders along wetlands and prairies. The Weapons-to-Wetlands Trail shows off migrating waterfowl or raptors, depending on the season.

*Fernald Preserve strives to serve as a community asset in the form of an undeveloped park with an emphasis on wildlife. Photo courtesy of Fernald Preserve Visitors Center.*

## FERNALD PRESERVE

**WHAT** Reclaimed grasslands

**WHERE** Fernald Preserve Visitors Center, 7400 Willey Rd., Hamilton, OH

**COST** Free. The Visitors Center is open 9 a.m.–5 p.m., Wednesday through Sunday. The nature trails are open 7 a.m. to dusk daily.

**PRO TIP** Stop at the Visitors Center to get info on the trails, current activities, and recent wildlife reports, and to learn about the site's history.

lm.doe.gov/Fernald/Sites.aspx

Any visit to the preserve should begin at the site's former warehouse-turned-award-winning Fernald Preserve Visitors Center. The center is the first building in the Buckeye state to receive Platinum certification from the US Green Building Council's Leadership in Energy and Environmental Design (LEED) rating system.

Exhibits narrate the site's historical timeline, opening with the chapter on Native Americans and moving through the arrival of settlers to the uranium-processing plant years and ultimately to the period of remediation as an undeveloped park, to the tune of $4.4 billion, and concluding with the ongoing maintenance and management of the land. But the preserve is best enjoyed outside, a pair of binoculars and camera in hand.

# 24 GARDEN OF HOPE

## Why does a replica of Jesus' tomb overlook Cincinnati?

Carved into the rock on a bluff overlooking a breathtaking sweep of Cincinnati is the tomb of Christ, an exact replica of the Garden Tomb of Jesus in Jerusalem.

### GARDEN OF HOPE

**WHAT** Replica tomb of Jesus

**WHERE** 699 Edgecliff St., Covington, KY

**COST** Free; freewill donation for guided tours gratefully accepted.

**PRO TIP** Be mindful where you're walking. Steps are uneven, and handrails aren't reliable. A parking lot is located past the Carpenter's Shop beyond the gravel road.

The tomb is one of the many religious features of the Garden of Hope, hidden away high atop a hill in Covington's west end. The Chapel of Dreams, modeled after a seventeenth-century Spanish Mission and topped by a trio of bells, is adorned with a stained-glass window from Cincinnati's Christ Church Cathedral. The Carpenter Shop has a highly detailed mural by local artist LeRoy Coastes that gives a glimpse of the lives of Palestinian carpenters, as well as carpenter tools donated by Israeli Prime Minister David Ben Gurion, supposedly eight hundred to nine hundred years old.

Additionally, the site contains a piece of Solomon's Temple, a stone from the Wailing Wall in Jerusalem, and stones from the River Jordan. Amidst a profusion of plants and flowers are trees and shrubs native to the Holy Land. Overlooking everything is an Italian-marble statue of Jesus delivering the Sermon on the Mount.

The Garden of Hope has been the crown jewel on this two-acre patch of land for more than sixty years. The brainchild of Rev. Morris H. Coers of Covington's Immanuel Baptist Church

(Above) *See the replica Tomb of Jesus at the Garden of Hope.* (Left) *The Garden of Hope is both a religious and a historic site. Photos courtesy of John Witt.*

(now shuttered), it opened on Palm Sunday in 1958, twenty years after the Holy Land visit that inspired its creation.

Regular church services take place in the Carpenter's Shop at 10:30 a.m. on Sunday; Sunrise Service takes place on Easter. Visitors may attend services or wander the grounds on their own any time, but to hear the stories of the miracles relating to the building of the garden or to get inside the tomb and other structures, you need to schedule a tour.

---

Steve Cummins, caretaker and tour guide since 2003, offers guided tours by appointment when weather permits. The Chapel of Dreams may be booked for small weddings.

# 25 GORMAN HERITAGE FARM

## Why are a gazillion sunflowers growing in Evendale fields?

From hunting grounds for the Shawnee, Miami, Mingo, and Chickasaw Indians to military roads pushing westward to a beloved family farm to an engaging outdoor classroom, the land beneath Gorman Heritage Farm has transformed over time with the imprint of many. One thing, however, has remained a constant: learning what the land can teach.

What do bees do in the wintertime? Why do sheep need haircuts? Where do eggs come from? When "school" is in session at this 122-acre educational center overlooking Millcreek Valley, students learn about history, food systems, life science, and geology. And when little hands dig into the nest to collect warm, fresh eggs, the lesson sticks.

In 1996, owners Jim and Dorothy Gorman turned their land over to the Cincinnati Nature Center, which began transforming it into an outdoor classroom. The farm is now owned by the Village of Evendale and managed by the Gorman Heritage Farm Foundation. The "curriculum" covers agriculture, nutrition, sustainability, and the environment.

Hiking trails, a children's garden, and educational programs—including storytime, hands-on activities, farm-to-

### GORMAN HERITAGE FARM

**WHAT** Lessons from the land

**WHERE** 10052 Reading Rd., Evendale, OH

**COST** $5/adults; $3/seniors and ages three–seventeen; free ages under three. Discounts for military.

**PRO TIP** Members receive free admission to Sunflower Festival and are invited to a special members-only event each year.

gormanfarm.org

*The fields at Gorman Heritage Farm are covered in sunflowers that shoot up just in time for the annual Sunflower Festival. Photo courtesy of Gorman Heritage Farm.*

table cooking classes, and more—make learning about farming and the land lively and entertaining.

Farm events include the annual late-summer Row by Row Dinner, with the menu based on the farm's chickens and produce and rounded out by desserts, wine, and beer. Music, dancing, silent and live auctions, and other fun and games are also part of the evening.

In early fall, just as fields of sunflowers are at their blooming best, the farm hosts its annual Sunflower Festival. Hayrides, sunflower and corn mazes, live music, food trucks, vendor booths, and pumpkins are part of this farm-fresh outing.

During Saturdays in October, there are free hayrides, a corn maze, and the opportunity to meet the farm animals and head into the field to cut your own sunflowers.

---

During the family friendly Sunflower Festival, the fields of Gorman Heritage Farm turn into a sea of yellow, with thousands upon thousands of sunflowers blooming. Festival-goers can cut their own sunflowers for a small fee.

# 26 MARY R. SCHIFF LIBRARY & ARCHIVES

## Why is one of the best views of the city framed by reference books on art and artists?

A reading room and terrace with a knock-your-socks-off view? Founded in 1881, the Mary R. Schiff Library & Archives at the Cincinnati Art Museum is not only a treasure trove of information about artists and art collections, but also the site of one of the most spectacular views of Cincinnati.

Located on the museum's third floor in the Longworth Wing, it looks west through a wall of windows that runs the length of the room and, even better, from a terrace where the view of downtown and Clifton Heights is completely unobstructed.

It is easy to overlook the space while exploring the galleries of the museum, where some sixty-seven thousand works of art take visitors on a journey through six thousand years of cultural heritage: African, Asian, and Native American; decorative arts and design; photography; American and European paintings and sculptures, fashion arts, and textiles; and so much more.

Still, make the time to visit what is considered the best art library in town, with a peerless collection of its own. Here, more than one hundred thousand items span six thousand years of art history, including decorative arts,

---

Open to the public for more than 130 years, the library occupies space that was once the Art Academy of Cincinnati. Cincinnati contemporary artist Jim Dine, whose Pinocchio sculpture greets museum guests, is a famous graduate.

*Mary R. Schiff Library & Archives at the Cincinnati Art Museum. Photo courtesy of Cincinnati Art Museum.*

fashion, and photography. Books, reference materials, videos/DVDs, periodicals, ephemera files, auction catalogs, online databases—the collection is exhaustive and still has room for a vast array of materials on Cincinnati art and artists.

But it's also an irresistible refuge for a time-out that comes with an unbeatable view.

## MARY R. SCHIFF LIBRARY & ARCHIVES

**WHAT** Room with a view

**WHERE** Cincinnati Art Museum, 953 Eden Park Dr.

**COST** General admission is free and parking in the museum lot is free.

**PRO TIP** Can't find something? Strike up a conversation with one of the highly qualified librarians. What you see represents a mere fraction of what is available.

cincinnatiartmuseum.org

# 27 FRISCH'S MAINLINER RESTAURANT

## Why does Big Boy have a sign with an airplane on it?

Here it is: The one, the only, the original Mainliner Restaurant, opened nearly eighty years ago by Dave Frisch of Frisch's Big Boy renown. The restaurant took its name from a United Air Lines' passenger airplane of the same name, which flew into nearby Lunken Airport.

Quicker than you can say "TS," it seared itself into the history books by becoming Cincinnati's first year-round drive-in restaurant.

Frisch had followed his father, Samuel Frisch, into the restaurant business. Dad opened Frisch Café in Cincinnati in 1905. It closed after five years, but he opened another restaurant, Frisch's Stag Lunch, ten years later in Norwood. Young Dave left high school to work at the restaurant. He did return to school, but before he graduated, Samuel Frisch died, leaving Dave and his brothers Reuben and Irving to run the restaurant.

That same year Dave went out on his own and opened the Frisch Café. He became a chain in 1938 with the opening of a second location, but when bankruptcy loomed that same year, he closed both cafés. Think of them as the preamble to the main event, the 1939 opening of the Mainliner, which became the first Frisch's Big Boy Restaurant in 1944.

### FRISCH'S MAINLINER RESTAURANT

**WHAT** Original Big Boy

**WHERE** 5760 Wooster Pike

**COST** Menu items vary.

**PRO TIP** While Frisch's Mainliner is no longer a drive-in eatery, its signage still features a replica of the famous aircraft, right down to the propellers.

frischs.com

(Above) *The interior and exterior of Frisch's Mainliner were recently remodeled. Photo courtesy of John Witt.* (Right) *The one and only Big Boy. Photo courtesy of Frisch's.*

Two years later, following an industry convention in California, Dave added something extra special to the menu: thinly packed and stacked patties on a burger bun. This double-decker delight already had the name "Big Boy," so Dave got permission to adopt the concept. He added his own flourish with a specially formulated tartar sauce and served up an overnight sensation.

Mmm. Big Boy brought in cars by the drove. The Mainliner had space for sixty cars, and hungry diners would order their food and munch down without ever stepping foot inside. Good thing. At the time, the restaurant had indoor dining space for only eight customers.

---

Big Boy visitors during the Dave Frisch years may have had their lunch served and table cleared by none other than the restaurant founder. It was Frisch's way of staying close to his customers.

# 28 BATTERY HOOPER AT THE JAMES A. RAMAGE CIVIL WAR MUSEUM

## How did a pile of dirt save a Cincinnati chapter of Civil War history?

It lay undisturbed on a swatch of land in Northern Kentucky for decades before being covered over with fill dirt in the 1940s, and it was this dirt that preserved Battery Hooper and a slice of Cincinnati-area Civil War history.

An earthen wall several feet high and located on a Fort Wright hilltop overlooking the Licking River Valley, Battery Hooper was one of twenty-eight such defensive strongholds built by Union forces in an eight-mile arc across Kenton and Campbell counties. The fortified cannon battery was named for industrialist William Hooper, who financed its 1861 construction. Today, it is one of only six remaining batteries.

In 1941, then-homeowners Fern and Sheldon Storer covered the site with soil to create a lawn. Fast forward sixty-one years to 2002: Fern Storer bequeathed her home and its fourteen rolling acres to the NKU Foundation, which, in turn, sold the property to the City of Fort Wright. The community swung into action to restore the battery and turn the home's first floor into the James A. Ramage Civil War Museum.

---

See Fern Storer's high-efficiency test kitchen, tricked out with a space-age refrigerator and stainless-steel cabinetry and wall tiles, on exhibit at the museum. From 1951–1976, she was food editor at the *Cincinnati Post*.

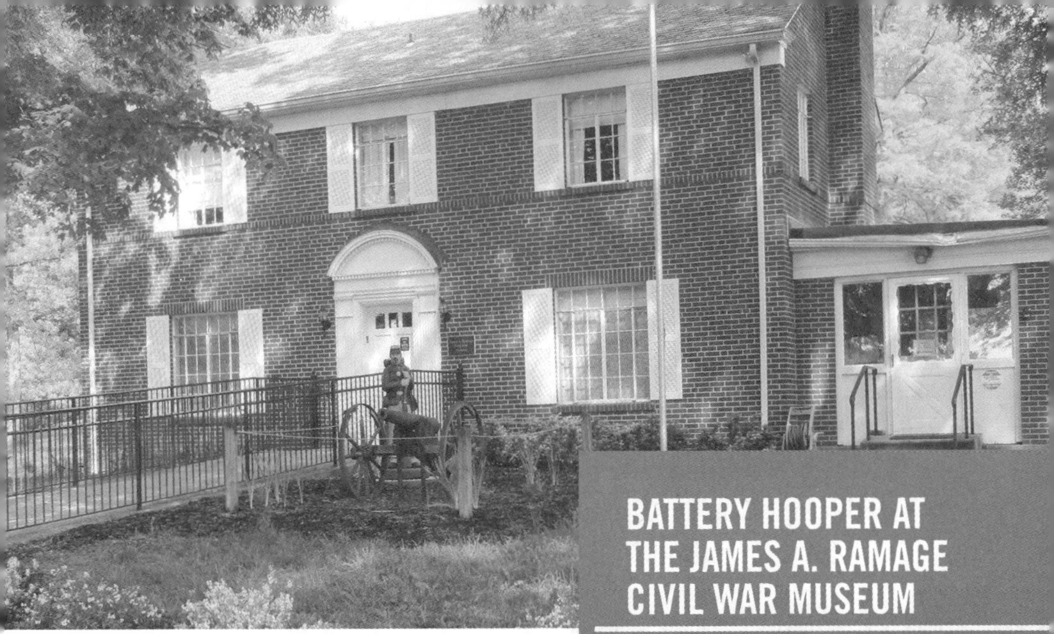

*Battery Hooper and James A. Ramage Civil War Museum preserves and interprets Northern Kentucky's unique role in the Civil War through archaeology, education and research. Photo courtesy of John Witt.*

## BATTERY HOOPER AT THE JAMES A. RAMAGE CIVIL WAR MUSEUM

**WHAT** Historic pile of dirt

**WHERE** 409 Kyles Lane, Fort Wright, KY

**COST** Free

**PRO TIP** Look for the portrait of General Lew Wallace. He would claim greater fame almost twenty years later as the author of Ben-Hur.

fortwright.com

But let's go back to the 1860s and the Civil War, specifically, September 10, 1862, when Confederate attack threatened the area. Under the command of General Lew Wallace of the Union Army, defenses were built and manned by twenty-two thousand Union troops and fifty thousand militia. A military pontoon bridge was built across the Ohio River for supplies. The would-be invaders, merely eight-thousand-strong, retreated.

Site digs have unearthed the remains of a Civil War–era powder magazine and dry well, as well as artifacts including Minnie balls and buckles. Inside the museum are displays of Confederate money, tintypes, artillery, a medical field bag, and a tribute to the Black Brigade. Fern Storer, author of *Recipes Remembered: A Collection of Modernized Nostalgia* and considered a pioneer of microwave cookery, is also remembered.

# 29 H. H. RICHARDSON MONUMENT

## How did a mini Stonehenge rise from the grounds of a Cincinnati park?

The recycled rubble on a rise at the south end of Burnet Woods in the University Heights/Clifton area and overlooking Martin Luther King Boulevard rocks a mini Stonehenge aesthetic.

### H. H. RICHARDSON MONUMENT

**WHAT** Cincinnati Stonehenge

**WHERE** Burnet Woods, 3251 Brookline Ave.

**COST** Free

**PRO TIP** A plaque at the monument provides more details about its installation and the key players involved in "Operation Resurrection."

cincinnatiparks.com

Located across the street from the University of Cincinnati's College of Design, Architecture, Art, and Planning, the H. H. Richardson Monument is a claptrap collection of pink granite blocks—fifty-one, no less!—that were once part of the window arches, columns, and walls of the old Cincinnati Chamber of Commerce Building.

Designed by H. H. himself, that castle-like building stood majestically at Fourth and Vine streets in downtown Cincinnati from the late 1880s until a fire destroyed it in 1911. In fact, the tallest of the monument blocks is the building's lintel stone bearing the engraving, "Chamber of Commerce," which was placed vertically to provide an impressive focal point for the monument.

The blocks didn't turn up at the park overnight. They were out-of-sight-out-of-mind for more than a half century before being rediscovered in 1967. Which is hard to believe, because they are chunky and bulky and weigh a combined total of eighty-four tons.

The H. H. Richardson Monument creates art with pieces of Cincinnati's old Chamber of Commerce building. Photo courtesy of John Witt.

The Chamber of Commerce Building was Henry Hobson Richardson's last design. Known for an architectural style he popularized, Richardsonian Romanesque, Richardson shares the hallowed company of Frank Lloyd Wright and Louis Sullivan among architecture's greats.

A design competition sponsored by the University of Cincinnati's architectural school as part of "Operation Resurrection" set the wheels in motion for the memorial installation in the ninety-acre Burnet Woods and the return of the stones. U.C. student Stephen Carter's design won, earning him a prize of three thousand dollars, put up by Cincinnati's Fleischmann family.

The stones, found in Cleves, Ohio, about twenty-five minutes from Cincinnati, were recovered and brought to the site. In 1972, about ninety years after the stones were first placed in Richardson's Chamber of Commerce Building, they were installed at the memorial site in Burnet Woods. The monument was dedicated in honor of Richardson, with "Operation Resurrection" deemed a smashing success.

# 30 HARLAN HUBBARD MURAL

### Why is a Great Depression–era mural adorning the stage at a local theatre?

Look up before, during, or after a production at the Otto M. Budig Theatre at The Carnegie and you will see a mural above the stage painted by Harlan Hubbard featuring four key figures relating to early area history and a hint of Cincinnati skyline.

While their identities aren't recorded, they are believed to be pioneer heroine Mary Draper Ingles, explorer Daniel Boone, lawyer-politician John G. Carlisle, and frontiersman Simon Kenton. Behind them, arms stretched heavenward, is an allegorical *Spirit of Covington*, which is also the name of the mural.

Hubbard was a writer, author, painter, and philosopher who loved being on the river and living off the land. Born in 1900 in Bellevue, Kentucky, Hubbard spent more years living away from the Cincinnati area than in it, but he remains one of the most celebrated and beloved artists in the region.

Two years before he died in 1988, he gave more than twenty of his paintings to the Behringer-Crawford; in fact, he allowed the director at the time to choose the pieces for what would become the museum's core collection of Harlan Hubbard works.

## HARLAN HUBBARD MURAL

**WHAT** The Spirit of Covington

**WHERE** The Carnegie, 1028 Scott St., Covington, KY

**COST** Free to see during gallery hours. Tickets for theatre productions vary.

**PRO TIP** Gallery hours are 12–5 p.m., Wednesday through Saturday, and always free. You won't be turned away should you arrive outside these hours.

thecarnegie.com

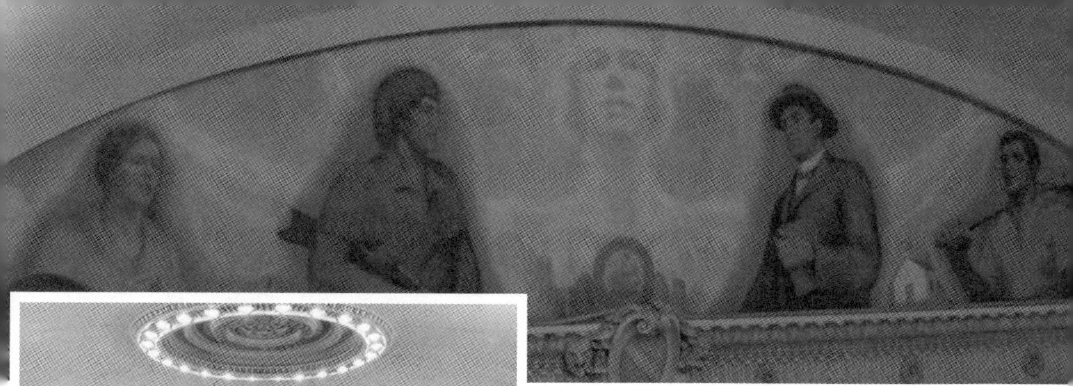

(Above) *Detail of Hubbard's "Spirit of Covington" mural. Photo courtesy of John Witt.* (Left) *Harlan Hubbard's "Spirit of Covington," a WPA-sponsored mural, hangs above the stage at The Carnegie. Photo courtesy of The Carnegie.*

In 1934, he painted a mural on the proscenium arch in the theatre addition of what was then the Covington Public Library. Built in 1904, it was one of many such buildings funded across the country by philanthropist Andrew Carnegie. Hubbard's mural was sponsored by the WPA (Works Progress Administration), a New Deal agency formed during the Great Depression.

When the library moved to a larger space in 1974, the building became a community arts center and began a slow slide into decrepitude. Restoration work began in 1999 and there, beneath more than a half century of grime, was Hubbard's mural. It was restored around 2005 and ready for its close-up when the Otto M. Budig Theatre held its grand opening in spring of 2006.

---

The Behringer-Crawford Museum has a permanent collection of sixty to seventy pieces created by Harlan Hubbard, including watercolors, woodcuts, oils, and acrylics. The art is rotated, but there are always pieces on display.

# 31 HISTORIC ANDERSON FERRY

## Where can you travel like the settlers?

Whether on wheels, hooves, or feet, the Historic Anderson Ferry has crossed the subject from one side of the Ohio River to the other, between Hebron, Kentucky, and Cincinnati, Ohio.

The Anderson Ferry began operations more than two hundred years ago in 1817, but the ferry business was already in full swing at this location. Nobody really knows quite how long, or when the crossings began, just that the business was purchased by another ferry operator.

Those early passengers would have boarded a ferry made of wood, with paddlewheels turning as horses walked along a treadmill. Today, the circa 1937 *Boone No. 7* represents the first steel-hulled ferry ever built, both for the Anderson Ferry company and to operate on western rivers. Its original steam engine has been replaced by a diesel engine, but the paddlewheels remain. The ferry relies on these to navigate the Ohio River current.

A succession of boats has shared the Boone name, beginning with *Boone No. 1,* built right after the Civil War. *Boone No. 4* is remembered as the last horse-drawn ferry, and *Boone No. 5* earned its place in history as the first steam ferry boat as well as the first that allowed passengers to drive onto the ferry on one end and drive off the other. Prior to

---

*Boone No. 7* entered service following the Great Flood of 1937. The Ohio River peaked in Cincinnati on January 26, nearly eighty feet higher than flood stage. Parts of the city remained submerged for nineteen days.

Historic Anderson Ferry is less than three miles from the Greater Cincinnati/Northern Kentucky International Airport and one mile from I-275. Photo courtesy of John Witt.

## HISTORIC ANDERSON FERRY

**WHAT** Passage into the past

**WHERE** One Anderson Ferry Rd., Cincinnati, OH and 4030 River Rd., Hebron, KY

**COST** $.50/foot pass; $5/car.

**PRO TIP** Bring cash; the ferry does not accept credit cards.

andersonferry.com

this, drivers had to pull on, then back off. *Boone No. 9* is of a much more recent vintage, having been purchased in 1993.

Listed on the National Register of Historic Places, the ferry carries cars and trucks, commuters and sightseers across the river and into the past. Once, during a Civil War re-enactment, it even carried soldiers on horseback. It is a lazy-day way to get from one state to another with several bonuses: it is scenic, saves time and fuel, and eliminates road rage.

# 32 GREATER CINCINNATI WATER WORKS

## Why are the world's largest steam engines located in Cincinnati?

At Greater Cincinnati Water Works' Old River Station, an architectural wonder that houses Ohio's first publicly owned water system, visitors are amazed to learn that, for fifty-seven years, four of the world's largest triple-expansion crank and flywheel water pumping steam engines helped move 120,000 gallons of water, every day. Even more astonishing is why the world's largest water pumping steam engines wound up in Cincinnati.

Two words: extreme fluctuations. The waters of the Ohio River can be as low as two feet and as high as seventy-five. Any steam engines built would have to be able to operate at both levels. Also, at the time the engines were built in 1906, a much smaller Cincinnati population could depend on having a three-week emergency supply of water, should the pumps break down. (Today there is a three-day backup supply.) Also, because the Little Miami River is an industrial stream, the plant is located just upstream from it to avoid having to treat that water.

"Visitors learn about the amazing ingenuity, creativity, and surprising hard work so many people contributed in order to provide a commonplace utility such as water, that today, is still yielding benefits," said Leland Hite, a retired engineer who provides monthly tours at Old River Station.

---

The RMS *Titanic*, built from 1909–1911, was also equipped with a triple-expansion steam engine, the most powerful one built, with 15,000 horsepower. Not that it helped.

The old Cincinnati Water Works (Old River Station) houses the four largest water pumping engines in the world at a height of one hundred four feet tall. Most of that height is beneath ground level and held within a circular pump house. The station was built 1898–1906 and was in service 1906–1963. The engines are no longer in service though the pump house still provides some use. Photo courtesy of John Witt.

## GREATER CINCINNATI WATER WORKS

**WHAT** Old River Station

**WHERE** 5651 Kellogg Ave. (GPS: Use 5695 Kellogg Ave.)

**COST** None, although donations are accepted.

**PRO TIP** Wear rubber-sole, closed-toe and heel shoes and bring a photo ID. Advise the tour guide if you suffer from vertigo, claustrophobia, or acrophobia so accommodations can be made for your tour.

cincinnatitriplesteam.org

Tours are typically held 9:30 a.m. to 12 p.m. the first Saturday of the month and include an up-close view of the 1,400-ton steam engines, which sit on a twenty-foot thick wood caisson twenty-six feet under the floor of the Ohio River in the engine house. The boiler house, coal storage area, and riverside coal handling dock remain at ground level. From here, you may spy the Intake Pier, located on one acre on the Kentucky side of the river. At tour's end, you get to climb the spiral staircase up five stories to return to the engine room, sitting beneath the domed ceiling.

# 33 HENRY FARNY PARK

## Why is a western mural painted on a fence in a Covington park?

There's a little piece of the American West in a pocket park in Covington's Old Seminary Square neighborhood. Located at the corner of Banklick and Robbins, the Henry Farny Park recalls the artist and illustrator born in 1847 who lived and worked for a time in Covington and Cincinnati. Farny became famous for his paintings that captured scenes of the life and culture of the American Indians and the vanishing West.

### HENRY FARNY PARK

**WHAT** The American West in Covington

**WHERE** 209–219 W. Robbins St., Covington, KY

**COST** Free

**PRO TIP** This park is all about appreciating the aesthetics of park and artist, so there are no picnic benches or other seating.

Farny had an affinity for American Indians that went back to his childhood in Pennsylvania, where he and his family lived after leaving Ribeauville, France, for America in 1853. The Farny home was located near a Seneca reservation.

Less than thirty years later, Farny embarked on the first of several trips west to pursue his interest, sketching and collecting artifacts as he went and eventually creating a body of oil paintings that today grace the walls of museums all over the country, including in Cincinnati.

---

Henry Farny was an early member of the Cincinnati Art Club, which was founded in 1890, the country's second oldest, continuously operating art club west of the Allegheny Mountains.

(Above) *Henry Farny Park recalls the artist who preserved the history of the American West in more than one hundred oil paintings.* (Left) *The sculpture in Henry Farny Park recalls the artist's distinctive signature. Photos courtesy of John Witt.*

The location of the park in Covington is fitting, as Farny lived at 1029-1031 Banklick Street from 1890 until his death in 1916. He painted one of his most recognizable and famous paintings, *The Song of the Talking Wire*, in 1904 while living here. Westside artist David Rice recalls this painting, on display at Cincinnati's Taft Museum of Art, in the mural he created on the park's picket-fence canvas.

West also created the park's sculpture centerpiece, that of Farny's Sioux signature (a dot within a circle), which appears on all his paintings. The park is colorful and utterly charming with stone walkway, metal horse and cactus silhouette sculptures, and trees and plants.

# 34 LUCKY CAT MUSEUM

## Why are two thousand Japanese "lucky charms" in a Cincinnati art gallery?

Artist Micha Robertson has a passion for cats. Not just any cats, but the maneki-neko, a whimsical Japanese figure that first appeared during the late Edo period (1603–1867), a time of peace and prosperity and economic growth in Japan.

In the United States, the maneki-neko are found in Japanese restaurants, a symbol of good luck and good fortune. These lucky cats are easy to spot because of their one raised or welcoming paw. In fact, the literal translation of maneki-neko is beckoning cat.

Robertson's zeal for the feline grew from a few figures scattered around her home to a massive collection numbering two thousand. They dominate her space at Essex Studios, an artist cooperative in Walnut Hills, peering from shelves, perching in shadowboxes, crowding curios, and posing in glass cases.

Among the figurines are wall hangings, wearables, books, teapots, and a collection of original works by Japanese artists rarely seen outside of that country.

The figures come in all sizes, shapes, materials, and colors, including litters of maneki-neko painted white with red ears. Some are plush, many are designer vinyl toys, and even more

---

Essex Studios is home to two hundred working artists, designers, and craftspeople: painters, photographers, sculptors, designers, jewelers, woodturners, printers, fused glass artists, theatre groups, ceramicists, luxury soap producers, potters, fashion designers, metalworkers, and more.

Hundreds and hundreds of maneki-neko of all description fill the shelves at the Lucky Cat Museum. Photo courtesy of John Witt.

## LUCKY CAT MUSEUM

**WHAT** Litters of lucky cats

**WHERE** Essex Place Studio, 2511 Essex Place Studio

**COST** Free

**PRO TIP** The Travel Channel series, Mysteries at the Museum, featured a segment about the Lucky Cat Museum in 2018.

luckycatmewseum.com

are ceramic. There are miniature figures, nesting sets, bobble-heads, a slowly spinning sparkly bank, a large wall clock keeping time with his tale, a Geisha, and even Garfield.

Pre–World War II maneki-neko include a miniature diorama of a toy/folk art vendor's storefront from 1929 and a set of original watercolors marked with the year 1931. Two Japanese slot machines are among "paws on" pieces visitors may play with, and Robertson happily demonstrates other interactive items.

In so quirky a collection, it might be challenging to spot the oddballs, but look for cats with extra limbs and extra faces and an antique tobacco pouch clasp featuring a lucky cat. According to Robertson, visitors tend to overlook the clasp in favor of the pouch and old pipes, assuming they are for opium.

# 35 MAGIC, A MEDIUM, AND MESSAGES FROM BEYOND

## Did a famous Cincinnati clairvoyant inspire her son to create the "Syco-Seer"?

A medium, an escape artist, the Magic 8-Ball. Is there a connection?

"Signs point to yes."

Laura C. Cooper Pruden (1855–1939) was a medium living and divining in Price Hill, who had achieved such stature in the spiritualism community of the 1920s and 1930s that she was once called out by none other than Harry Houdini. The escape artist extraordinaire and national president, from 1917 to 1926, of the oldest fraternal magic organization in the world, the Society of American Magicians, had no patience for charlatans. Houdini proclaimed his magic was based on skill and sheer physical strength.

Pruden not only conducted seances in the Cincinnati area, including at Covington's Baker Hunt home, but also excelled as a slate-writer. In fact, Pruden invented the Psycho-Slate, a chalkboard enclosed in a box that would allegedly reveal answers from the spectral realm, as a tool to aid in her predictions. How she carried this off is a question for another device soon to be invented and also born of the psychic realm.

Pruden had a son named Albert Carter (1888–1948) and, in matters of mysticism, he didn't fall far from the tree, or

---

Spring Grove Cemetery and Arboretum offers a variety of tours, including Twilight Tours, Early Morning Bird Walks, and History Tours by horse-drawn carriage, tram tours, and walkabouts, plus a summer concert series.

*At the end of the family line, poor Albert C. Carter has no footstone. Albert's brother, George C. Mosser, and mother, Laura C. Cooper Pruden, must have thought ahead. Photo courtesy of John Witt.*

divining rod, in this case. Carter is credited with inventing the catchily-named Syco-Seer, a soothsayer in a tube that provided straightforward "yes" or "no" answers to fortune-seekers. It would lead to the invention of one of the most enduring and famous toys ever made.

Carter applied for a patent for his invention (and died shortly before it was granted), but it was two other Cincinnatians (Max Levinson and Abe Bookman and their company, Alabe Crafts) who finetuned the foretelling device that eventually evolved into that awesome oracle known as the Magic 8-Ball.

Mother and son are now residents of Spring Grove Cemetery, buried side by side. One wonders if there is any communication beyond the graves.

"My sources say no."

## MAGIC, A MEDIUM, AND MESSAGES FROM BEYOND

**WHAT** Gravesites of Laura C. Cooper Pruden and Albert C. Carter

**WHERE** Spring Grove Cemetery, 4521 Spring Grove Ave.

**COST** Free

**PRO TIP** Find the Psycho-Slate and Syco-Seer inventors in Section 124, Lot 235 (Spaces 2 and 3). Alas, Albert has no stone, but he rests to the right of his mother.

springgrove.org

# 36 MARTHA, LAST PASSENGER PIGEON

## Why is world's last passenger pigeon memorialized in Cincinnati?

There was once a bird species known for its sustained speed, noisy chatter, and spectacular migratory flights.

The species numbered in the billions, "countless numbers," as French explorer and founder of Quebec Samuel de Champlain noted in 1605. Later that century, influential New England Puritan minister Cotton Mather described a flight, estimating the width to stretch over a mile or so and taking several hours to pass overhead, during which time the sky would be darkened.

The passenger pigeon.

The species went from extravagant numbers to extinct in only fifty years, when aggressive slaughter began in 1850. By 1900, it was pretty much over for passenger pigeons in the wild.

A few survived in captivity, including Martha (named for Martha Washington), who was living at the Cincinnati Zoo. By 1910, Martha was the last of her kind. She died on September 1, 1914, effectively closing the books on a species that was the most abundant bird in North America, making up an incredible 25 to 40 percent of the total bird population of the United States, and possibly the world.

### MARTHA, LAST PASSENGER PIGEON

**WHAT** Bronze bird memorial

**WHERE** Cincinnati Zoo, 3400 Vine St.

**COST** $17/adults; $12/seniors, children (online).

**PRO TIP** The zoo offers free admission to all members of the military (active and retired) on Memorial Day, July 4th, and Veteran's Day with government-issued ID.

cincinnatizoo.org

(Left) *The Memorial Building, saved due to the efforts of artist John Ruthven and former zoo director Ed Maruska, remembers Martha and all extinct specials.* (Right) *The bronze memorial dedicated to Martha sits outside near the entrance of the aviary pagoda. Photos courtesy of the Cincinnati Zoo & Botanical Garden.*

Visitors to the Cincinnati Zoo will find the bronze statue memorializing Martha and the passenger pigeon at the zoo's last remaining Japanese pagoda-style building, an early aviary (and National Historic Landmark) built in 1875. Today it is called the Memorial Building.

In 2014, in commemoration of the 100th anniversary of Martha's death, the building was renovated to create an educational exhibit that broadens the scope of the passenger pigeon saga to encompass modern wildlife conservation efforts.

See passenger pigeon sculptures carved by Gary Denzler, a reprint of John J. Audubon's passenger pigeon hand-colored engraving from *Birds of America*, and a large reproduction of John Ruthven's 2013 painting of *Martha, the Last Passenger Pigeon*, among displays narrating stories of native species that were nearly lost and examples of efforts to save threatened species today.

---

Founded in 1873 by German immigrant Andrew Erkenbrecher, the Cincinnati Zoo & Botanical Gardens is the second oldest zoo in the country. It is also the greenest zoo in America, leading the zoo world in sustainability practices.

# 37 HERITAGE VILLAGE MUSEUM AND EDUCATIONAL CENTER

### Where is time travel routinely encouraged?

In a small, two-room office built before the Civil War, a collection of medical instruments narrates a sometimes-scary story of nineteenth-century medicine.

A general store built following the Civil War is stocked with goods for yesteryear shoppers.

A circa 1891 schoolhouse recalls how the three Rs were part of a curriculum that also included lessons in industry, integrity, modesty, love, service, and patriotism for students of Delhi Township School District No 3.

Walking into the Heritage Village Museum and Educational Center in Sharon Woods, a community of thirteen historic structures saved from destruction, is to time-travel back to 1800s rural Southwest Ohio. With its heavily forested grounds, the park itself helps usher visitors into the simpler times of a century or two ago.

The village is all about visitors going hands-on and is abuzz with activities, special exhibits, and events throughout the year: guided tours with interpreters in period dress; busy summer daycamps with themes including Native Americans,

---

For six nights every October, Heritage Village Museum and Educational Center transforms into a Haunted Village with trick-or-treating, face painting, horse-drawn wagon rides, and other activities, along with appearances by ghouls, witches, and even a mad scientist.

A photograph of students and their teacher, William Chidlaw, at Myers District School (Delhi Township School District. No. 3), circa early 1900s. Photo courtesy of Heritage Village Museum and Educational Center.

## HERITAGE VILLAGE MUSEUM AND EDUCATIONAL CENTER

**WHAT** Nineteenth-century village

**WHERE** Sharon Woods, 11450 Lebanon Rd., Sharonville, OH

**COST** $5/guided tours; $3/self-guided tours (outside of buildings only).

**PRO TIP** Although no evidence has been found to support the claims, many believe the village is haunted. Ghost hunters may wish to pack an EVP recorder or EMF meter, just in case.

heritagevillagecincinnati.org

archaeology, and pioneers; period dinners, like a hearth-cooked meal prepared in the village's Kemper Kitchen straight from an 1804 menu; and a First Person Program Series that resurrects notable figures from the past.

A Civil War Weekend in the summer gathers soldiers, citizens, and cavalry at the village for daily battles, living history demos in the historic buildings, interactive fun, and a chance to meet presidents Abraham Lincoln and Jefferson Davis.

December is packed with events, including breakfast and photo ops with Father Christmas; Holly Days, a nineteenth-century holiday celebration with storytelling, music, crafts, and more; and Train Days, a chance to break from holiday hubbub to see the Great Circle Line & Points North O-Scale Model Railway that gets set up during Holly Days.

# 38 MARY M. EMERY MEMORIAL CARILLON

**Where can you enjoy a free concert outdoors in the dead of winter?**

Neither snow nor rain nor heat nor gloom of night keeps the carillon concerts from ringing out from the free-standing bell tower rising over Dogwood Park in the Village of Mariemont.

Every Sunday and major holiday, the carillonneur climbs the nearly eighty steps to the playing room, located directly beneath the bell chamber, and performs an hour-long recital, masterfully eliciting melodies from delicate to thunderous.

The Mary M. Emery Memorial Carillon is owned (and the recitals and upkeep of the instrument funded) by the Thomas J. Emery Memorial, a non-profit foundation set up in 1925 by Mary Emery, the founder of the Village of Mariemont, in memory of her late husband.

### MARY M. EMERY MEMORIAL CARILLON

**WHAT** Carillon concerts

**WHERE** Dogwood Park, 3721 Pleasant St., Mariemont, OH

**COST** Free

**PRO TIP** Concerts are at 7 p.m. on Sundays during the summer; 4 p.m. the rest of the year; and 2 p.m. on major holidays.

mariemont.org

"Hear Ye! Hear Ye!" Mariemont is among a dozen or so towns in America with a town crier, a role (and tradition) that dates back to biblical times. Official duties include opening the town meeting and leading the Memorial Day Parade.

*The carillon is known to be a very expressive instrument and the Mary M. Emery Memorial Carillon does not disappoint. Photo courtesy of John Witt.*

One of the first planned communities in the United States, Mariemont was established nearly a century ago in 1923 when Emery, one of the nation's wealthiest women, broke ground with her silver spade. (The spade is on display in the village's municipal building.)

The village evokes the charm of a picture-postcard English garden neighborhood and takes its name from Emery's Rhode Island estate. It is a National Historic Landmark community with quiet tree-lined streets, Tudor-style buildings, fifty acres of parkland, tennis courts, swimming pools, and the bell tower. Dedicated to the youth of Mariemont in 1929, the campanile was given in Emery's honor by her sister, Isabella Hopkins.

One of only 180 carillons in North America, the Mary M. Emery Memorial Carillon has forty-nine bells covering a musical range of just over four octaves. The largest bell, the bourdon, weighs a hefty 4,900 pounds.

Recitals feature everything from English folk songs to American spirituals to classical music. Tours of the carillon, including the keyboard area and the actual bells, are available following the Sunday concerts and upon request with advance notice. All programs play rain or shine or snow.

# 39 HARRIET BEECHER STOWE HOUSE

## What does "the little woman who wrote the book" President Lincoln allegedly said "made this great war" have to do with a travel guide?

The author of one of the most significant and enduring books ever written, *Uncle Tom's Cabin*, lived in Cincinnati's Walnut Hills neighborhood for nearly twenty years, from 1832 to the early 1850s, and based her watershed novel on experiences that took place here.

Harriet Beecher Stowe (1811–1896) spent years in a house many Cincinnatians drive past hundreds of times, given its location at the corner of Martin Luther King Boulevard and Gilbert Avenue, but have no idea the abolitionist writer lived here for four years prior to her 1936 marriage to Calvin Stowe. She was a frequent visitor after.

Beecher Stowe's famous father, Rev. Lyman Beecher, moved his family to the house in 1832 when he accepted the position of president of Lane Theological Seminary. A quick stroll from the house, the seminary was the site of what were most likely the first public debates about slavery.

Beecher's house was a center for discussion and debate about abolitionism in the 1830s and 1840s. At its heart and

---

"The Abolitionists Walking Tour: Walnut Hills" includes the Walnut Hills Presbyterian Church, Calvin and Harriet Beecher Stowe House (no longer standing), Lane Theological Seminary (only steps remain), the Elizabeth Blackwell House (first female physician in the United States), and the Harriet Beecher Stowe House.

*The Harriet Beecher Stowe House is on the National Underground Railroad Network to Freedom. Photo courtesy of John Witt.*

## HARRIET BEECHER STOWE HOUSE

**WHAT** Famous abolitionists's home

**WHERE** 2950 Gilbert Ave.

**COST** $4 for adults, $2 for children ages six–eighteen, children five and under are free.

**PRO TIP** The home is currently in the midst of a restoration process in conjunction with the Ohio History Connection.

stowehousecincy.org

soul was Harriet herself, a catalyst for social change whose goal with the 1852 publication of her book was to “write something that would make this whole nation feel what an accursed thing slavery is.”

One hundred years after the family lived here, their home had transformed into an African American boarding house and tavern. Walnut Hills in the 1930s was a vibrant black business district, and the Beechers’ former residence was now included in the *Negro Motorist Green Book*, its author another catalyst for social change.

Postal carrier Victor Hugo Green created the guidebook for African American travelers. Augmented by field reports from fellow postal carriers across the country, it eventually included thousands of establishments all over the United States known to be either black-owned or verified non-discriminatory. The place that influenced Beecher Stowe, now a tavern, was among the listings.

# 40 HIDDEN STAIRCASE

## Why are steps hidden in the brush at the overlook in Devou Park?

One of the most glorious and photogenic views of downtown Cincinnati and Covington and the Ohio River flowing between these two cities is known by anyone growing up in the area.

It is from the Devou Memorial Overlook at Drees Pavilion in Covington's Devou Park, a breathtaking picture postcard of Cincinnati's famed skyline of skyscrapers, stadiums, and variously colored bridges arching over the river toward the banks of Covington, its riverside structures, church steeples, and parkland. And it draws visitors, wedding parties, walkers, and artists like a magnet.

Just east of the overlook is a walking trail that leads to a staircase hidden by clumps of honeysuckle, massive trees, and brush. Follow a short set of steps with handrail to a flat area. This is the opening to the staircase that shoots off into the woods. There is no handrail here, and walking can be tricky, sometimes even treacherous as some of the steps are broken, uneven, and covered with branches, tangled underbrush, and other debris.

Follow the steps, interspersed with packed ground, down a zigzagging path. At the end of the line? A quiet neighborhood of houses lined up neatly along Western Avenue. A few steps

### HIDDEN STAIRCASE

**WHAT** A walk on the wild side

**WHERE** Devou Park, Devou Dr., Park Hills, KY

**COST** Free

**PRO TIP** The staircase is cut into the woods so it is heavily covered with brush, etc., spring through summer, making a temperate winter day the best and least buggy time to hike the steps.

covingtonky.gov/visitors/parks/devou-park

*The hidden staircase disappears into the woods of Devou Park. Photos courtesy of John Witt.*

away, at the intersection of Western and Devou Drive, the road leads right back into Devou Park at its Covington entrance, past Haven Gillespie Blvd. and returning to the Drees Pavilion.

No one seems to know what purpose the staircase serves, but for residents of Western Avenue and surrounding neighborhood, it is a huge convenience to quickly reach one of the greatest views in town, if you can make it up the 273 steps.

---

The Devou Golf and Event Center opened in 2017 with new clubhouse and bar and grill. The golf course opened originally in 1922. Today, it is certified as an Audubon Cooperative Sanctuary by Audubon International.

# 41 FLORENCE FREEDOM

## Where does "If you build it, he will come" happen?

Running the bases, catching a fireworks show, dressing up like a princess or superhero, and, of course, watching a Florence Freedom home game at its high-energy stadium is on the summer schedule for legions of fans in the Greater Cincinnati area.

What visitors to the ballpark may not know is that developing an independent professional baseball league was the brainchild of a few guys back in 1992–1993, who thought it would be great to bring professional baseball to places that didn't have a softball's chance in, well, you get the point—of ever having affiliated professional baseball show up on their community's doorstep.

Voila: the Frontier League. Fast-forward to the 2002 post-season and the team—previously named the Erie Sailors, Johnstown Steal, and Johnstown Johnnies— was sold and moved to Florence, Kentucky. The renamed Florence Freedom didn't play their 2003 home games in Florence, however. They played at a field north of Cincinnati while waiting for their new home to be built.

In 2004, Champion Window Field Stadium opened, and the Freedom, and the league itself, have celebrated many firsts, including the first time the Frontier League attracted more than 1.1 million fans (2003) and the first game sold out for the Freedom (2007).

### FLORENCE FREEDOM

**WHAT** On-field ball game or batting practice

**WHERE** UC Health Stadium, 7950 Freedom Way, Florence, KY

**COST** Prices vary for single game tickets and the field experiences.

**PRO TIP** The meeting space set-up fee is waived for groups buying the Executive "Field of Dreams" package.

florencefreedom.com

(Above) *Florence Freedom is all about fun and games for all. Photo courtesy of John Witt.* (Left) *Florence Freedom is a member of the twelve-team Independent Frontier League, composed of teams from Kentucky, Ohio, Indiana, Illinois, Michigan, Missouri and Pennsylvania. Photo courtesy of Justine Krieg courtesy of Florence Freedom.*

Now named the UC Health Stadium, the ballpark continues to be a magnet for fans of the sport and of fun in general. It also has a stupendous perk that remains under the radar with its Florence Freedom Executive "Field of Dreams" package. (Yes, it is as good as it sounds.)

The stadium hosts meetings, training classes, and team building during the day. For participating groups, there is an opportunity to add an on-field experience like batting practice or a softball or kickball game, right on the field of the Defending Frontier League West Division Champions. And if a player is home, he can be added.

---

The Frontier League is independent of Major League Baseball, but thirty-four players have been called up to MLB, including former Florence Freedom players Steve Delabar, Chris Jakubauskas, Jorge Marban, and Stephen Cardullo.

# 42 JANE'S SADDLEBAG

## Why is this twenty-one-acre family playground named for horse tack?

With its Kids Village and Kids Playland, corn pit, petting zoo, and life-size replica of a 1700s flatboat, Jane's Saddlebag is the very definition of fresh-air family fun. And not just for the kiddos. Mom and Dad can sample gold medalist JSB Reserve Bourbon or sip regional wines at the Whine Shoppe, and everyone can rummage among the goodies at Wyatt's General Store to pick out souvenirs.

Far from city commotion and sheltered amidst acres of trees, this supersized playground stretches out along the banks of the Ohio River and stands ready to entertain. Shout "ahoy!" from the pirate ship. Peek inside an Indian Longhouse. Meet the farm's goats, chickens, and pigs. Snap a selfie in the jail cell. Bounce along the grounds on a haywagon ride.

Jane's is where kids and parents can play together Fridays through Sundays, April through October, and during special events, like the August Kids Festival and October's Halloween Fall Fest with trick-or-treating and Haunted Kids Village. (Both are free-admission.)

Jane's also hosts an annual wine festival and arts and crafts show and Friday night steak dinners and cruise-ins (selected dates). Speaking of, plan a meal stop at the restaurant during your visit. Does it feel like you just walked into grandma's

---

Nearby, fifteen or so bison roam the grounds of Kentucky State Park treasure, Big Bone Lick State Historic Site. Its redesigned museum has all-new exhibits on paleontology, Ordovician geology, ice age mammals, and Native American history.

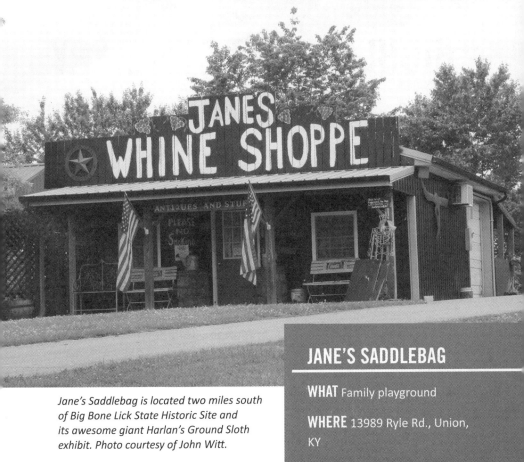

*Jane's Saddlebag is located two miles south of Big Bone Lick State Historic Site and its awesome giant Harlan's Ground Sloth exhibit. Photo courtesy of John Witt.*

## JANE'S SADDLEBAG

**WHAT** Family playground

**WHERE** 13989 Ryle Rd., Union, KY

**COST** No admission. Some activities have a small fee.

**PRO TIP** Tickets required for the hayride, petting zoo, and Kids Playland can be purchased at Wyatt's General Store.

janessaddlebag.com

kitchen? That was the intent when the family that owns Jane's Saddlebag set up housekeeping. Everyone can go elbows-off-the-table for a homecooked meal of Wooly Mammoth burgers or turkey 'n' dressing, among other entrées, and finish it off with a Glacial Smore, apple blossom, or some other confection.

By the way, Jane was the original owner of the land, and "saddlebag" refers to that rural style of home whose two rooms share a chimney, not the pouches that hang from a saddle on the back of a horse.

# 43 HIGHLAND PET CEMETERY

## Is "We love you Bugar" an appropriate epitaph for a tombstone?

Sugar, Honey, Trouble, Biscuit, Baby.

These names are not what one would typically see on a stroll through the cemetery, but this is not the final resting place for people but for pets, as beloved a family member (or in some cases even more so) than a blood relative.

The inscriptions on the tombstones illustrate the love and unabashed devotion the humans had for their fur babies: "Mikie, beloved friend of Karen and soulmate of Michael." "Naomi, guiding force of love and support, constant friend and companion, gratitude and love forever." "Simon, a pure heart, a real friend, we will always love you."

Opened in 1995, the Highland Pet Cemetery is a peaceful patch of green tucked at the back of Highland Cemetery in Fort Mitchell. The entrance

### HIGHLAND PET CEMETERY

**WHAT** Memorial pet park

**WHERE** Highland Cemetery, 2167 Dixie Highway, Fort Mitchell, KY

**COST** Free to visit. Trails are free.

**PRO TIP** To reach the Nature Trail, enter the cemetery and take all right-hand turns, passing a lake on the right to the parking lot at the trail entrance.

highlandcemeterysite.wordpress.com

---

Wildflowers, waterfalls, wooded tranquility: Highland Cemetery has four miles of nature trails weaving through 150 acres, a wildlife viewing idyll with wrens, great horned owls, bluebirds, and other species.

(Top) *Perpetual care for that special family member is offered at Highland Pet Cemetery.*
(Above) *The official greeters at the Highland Pet Cemetery. Photos courtesy of John Witt.*

is marked with an etched landscape boulder flanked by several statue-sentinels, including a bunny, shaggy sheep dog, and a hound dog gripping a flower basket in its mouth. A stone nearby reads: "This stone is placed in memory of animals abused and neglected in life," placed at the cemetery by Paws To Remember, a pet memorial service whose mission is to provide grief support and memorialization to pet owners.

But this is a place that knows only peace and comfort for the animals laid to rest here.

With evergreens and pink blossoming trees edging the grounds, the cemetery is a dignified sanctuary, secluded and sun-dappled. Fresh flowers mark some of the gravesites, showing these cherished chums have not been forgotten.

The cemetery is located past the chapel, lake, and crypt area and beyond the Highland Cemetery Nature Trail and trail entrance.

**CAREW TOWER OBSERVATION DECK** (page 8)

**CINCINNATI ART MUSEUM** (page 12 and 54)

**GARDEN OF HOPE** (page 50)

**GLENWOOD GARDENS** (page 30)

**HAIL DARK AESTHETICS** (page 34)

Turkey
Feathers
$15

**HISTORIC ANDERSON FERRY** (page 64)

**H. H. RICHARDSON MONUMENT** (page 60)

NO STOPPING PARKING
ANY TIME
TOW ZONE

MUSHROOM HOUSE (page 188)

516

**PAINTED LADIES** (page174)

**PARTY SOURCE SPIRITS LIBRARY** (page 110)

**PYRAMID HILL SCULPTURE PARK & MUSEUM** (page 154)

**RIVERSIDE DRIVE STATUE TOUR** (page 172)

**GREATER CINCINNATI WATER WORKS** (page 66)

# 44 LICKING RIVER GREENWAY & TRAILS

**Why are flocks of birds painted on a box in an empty field?**

## LICKING RIVER GREENWAY & TRAILS

**WHAT** River respite

**WHERE** Licking River Greenway & Trails: Trail Entrance, Corner of Levassor Place and Eastern Ave., Covington, KY

**COST** Free

**PRO TIP** Besides the main Trail Entrance, other access points include the dead end of East 16th St., Clayton-Meyer Park, and behind Randolph Park in Covington.

covingtonky.gov
facebook.com/lrgtrails

Flocks of birds soar into the sky. Children swing into the air in silhouette. A riverside community basks in brilliant sunshine.

Along sections of the Licking River Greenway & Trails, a multi-phase, multiuse urban trail through the Licking River corridor in Covington, brightly painted murals splashed across gatewells (structures along the levee that regulate water flow) add to the scenic splendor of the wooded riverscape.

The seventeen murals were inspired by the idea of energy in its many forms (recreational, emotional, transformational,

From No. 1, artist Susan Mahan's *River Morning Patchwork*, through No. 17, Marina Garcia Gamez's *A Wishful World, Mix and Melt Colors*, the series of Licking River murals, created through a partnership between ArtWorks and SkywardNKY, celebrates the river.

(Above) *The Licking River Greenway is a multi-phase project to build an interconnected urban trail through the Licking River corridor.* (Right) *A flock of birds take flight on the Licking River Greenway. Photos courtesy of John Witt.*

the natural environment, people and community, and more) and pay tribute to the Licking River, celebrate its ecosystems, and laud the hikers, walkers, bikers, and nature lovers who enjoy the river.

The murals tell only part of the story of the trailway system. Trails meander along Clayton-Meyer and Randolph parks, into the woods, atop the levee, and beside city streets as they follow the flow of the Licking River on its way to meet up with the Ohio River. Once completed, the trail system will span about four miles.

The creation and linking of these nature, paved, and water trails have sparked habitat restoration, an ecologically healthy landscape where native plants can thrive, riverbank stabilization, the development of a Blueway plan to establish locations for kayaking and canoeing enthusiasts, beautification projects like the murals and lots of community synergy, and esprit de corps.

The trails are peaceful and, in some spots, pristine, their rugged beauty enhanced by the colorful murals. For paddlers, there are three access points: Mike Fink's Landing in Covington, Forty-Seventh and Decoursey in Latonia, and Licking from Fredrick's Landing in Wilder.

# 45 PARTY SOURCE SPIRITS LIBRARY

**At what library can you check out an eighty-proof liquor?**

Some people love walking into a library because of the smell of the books. At the Party Source Spirits Library, smelling is a key part of the experience, along with swirling, sipping, swishing, and swallowing. That's because the volumes contained within this library aren't numbered in pages, but in ounces.

The Party Source is already a grown-up wonderland, with its high-tech filling and canning station that specializes in fresh local and regional craft beer, private-barrel whiskeys, clubby cigar room, gourmet cheese cases, and tasting events. The spirits library, housed in dignified cabinetry whose backlit shelves present the bottles in a glow of come-hither illumination, adds another dimension of sophistication to an outing to pick up a bottle of booze.

About five hundred bottles fill the library, but don't look for a Dewey Decimal System of organization here; spirits are arrayed by type, and the variety and availability changes as new items are introduced.

The most expensive labels ring in at around $150. Tastings for these are limited to the most serious of patrons. Unusual spirits include the complex and richly flavored Ancho Reyes Chili Poblano Liqueur, made with chilis native to Puebla,

---

Have a special occasion? The Party Source offers free personalized engraving on select products at no charge. Customize up to three lines on the front of the bottle; bottles are ready in about ten business days.

*Here's your chance to sample the really good stuff: The Party Source Spirits Library. Photo courtesy of John Witt.*

## THE PARTY SOURCE SPIRITS LIBRARY

**WHAT** Liquor library

**WHERE** 95 Riviera Dr, Bellevue, KY

**COST** Free

**PRO TIP** Visitors may indulge their most top-shelf whims with two to four tastings, with each sampling measuring a quarter of an ounce.

thepartysource.com

Mexico (and a real stalwart at eighty proof), and chareau's small-batch aloe liqueur, its natural sweetness giving way to a generous floral element and clean taste.

Also unusual but swiftly moving toward the top of the bestseller list is bacon-flavored bourbon, a sublime pairing of two gastronomically pleasing powerhouses. Just for fun is a line of whiskeys that suggest dessert: caramel turtle, chocolate mint, bourbon ball.

The Tasting Bar is open from noon until 8 p.m., but liquor laws being among the most convoluted, the bar can remain open only for four continuous hours. If you show up and the bar is unattended, don't worry: The librarian will reopen following a short break.

# 46 MEMORIAL GROVES

**Why is a stone tome lying open in a grove of trees in Eden Park?**

Pioneers, presidents, heroes, and authors are all remembered in several groves in Eden Park that were planted as early as 1876.

The largest is Presidential Grove, established on April 27, 1882, during Cincinnati's first Arbor Day celebration. A white oak tree planted in memory of President George Washington, its substantial girth attesting to its decades of noble growth, is joined by a variety of trees honoring the other nineteen US presidents who had served up to that time. Number twenty, a rugged burr oak, pays homage to James A. Garfield, struck down in 1881 by Charles J. Guiteaua, who had been stalking him for months.

The tradition of planting trees for the chief executive has continued through the years, but now presidents (or their family or descendants) get to select the type of tree they want once they leave office. For instance, President

## MEMORIAL GROVES

**WHAT** Stands of tagged trees

**WHERE** Eden Park (south, east, and west of the water tower)

**COST** Free

**PRO TIP** Park at the Memorial Grove entrance and walk right in. A set of steps also leads uphill to the groves from Krohn Conservatory.

cincinnatiparks.com

---

The granite boulders that once marked the trees in Presidential Grove were mostly removed because they resembled gravestones. Tree tags now identify the president, years in office, and type of tree.

(Above) *Forty-four trees, the majority of which are a species of oak, commemorate US Presidents at Eden Park's Memorial Groves.* (Left) *Authors Grove is marked by an open book resting on a pedestal. Photos courtesy of John Witt.*

Ronald Reagan elected an American sycamore. President Bush, both forty-one and forty-three, selected the D.D. Blanchard magnolia. It was a swamp white oak for President Bill Clinton, and President Barack Obama opted for a burr oak.

South of the Presidential Grove is Pioneers Grove (also planted as part of the 1882 Arbor Day celebration), where thirty-six deciduous trees honor Cincinnati's pioneers and early settlers. In Authors Grove, thirty-five trees planted that same year recall "philosophers, poets, statesmen, scientists, and various other honored representatives in the paths of literature." This stand of trees, selected by Cincinnati Public School students, is marked with a book carved in a granite block perched atop a column.

Six years before these three groves were planted, Heroes Grove was established on April 27, 1876. It was a centennial commemoration of the hero-patriots of the Revolutionary War, with thirty-five trees, all sturdy oaks, brought from the Valley Forge, Pennsylvania, battlefield.

The groves are connected by paved walkways commemorating park stewards, commissioners, and Park Foundation presidents.

# 47 LINCK BREWERY TUNNELS

### Why is Cincinnati's brewing heritage buried thirty feet underground?

More than 150 years ago, talented construction workers in the mid-to late-1800s built massive stone chambers with arched ceilings beneath the streets of Cincinnati's historic Over-The-Rhine neighborhood. The area, now known as OTR, had been heavily settled by German immigrants, who made it the hub of Cincinnati's beer-brewing industry. Call it a lager labyrinth, if you will. Dozens of brewers used this vast network of tunnels thirty to forty feet belowground to keep their beer cold.

In the fall of 2016, construction got underway for OTR's Epicurean Mercantile Co., an urban grocery known as EMC among the locals. The builders discovered the tunnels from the old Linck Brewery. Not just the vaulted tunnels, but wooden fermentation tanks, too, a rare and unexpected treasure.

In the mid-1850s, the Linck Brewery sat on what is

## THE LINCK BREWERY TUNNELS

**WHAT** Underground beer tunnels

**WHERE** Tours begin at 1818 Race St.

**COST** $25 (tickets may be purchased online at www.AmericanLegacyTours.com).

**PRO TIP** The tunnels are located across from Findlay Market, Cincinnati's oldest, liveliest, and most beloved public market, in operation since 1852.

---

The entrance to the tunnels is behind a locked-door in the EMC building and is accessible only on American Legacy's Under the Market Tour.

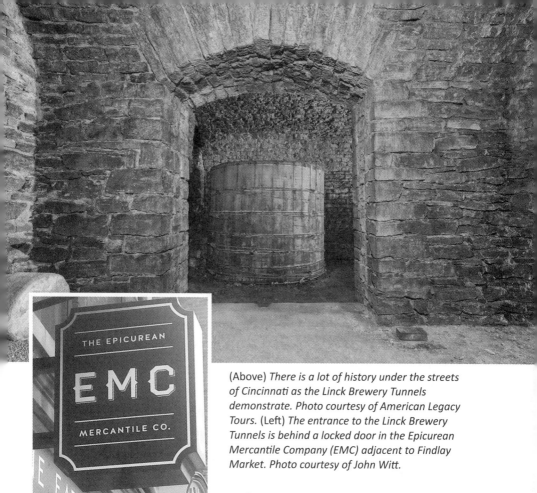

(Above) *There is a lot of history under the streets of Cincinnati as the Linck Brewery Tunnels demonstrate. Photo courtesy of American Legacy Tours.* (Left) *The entrance to the Linck Brewery Tunnels is behind a locked door in the Epicurean Mercantile Company (EMC) adjacent to Findlay Market. Photo courtesy of John Witt.*

today McMicken Avenue, not far from where the opening of the tunnels was discovered at 1818 Race Street. The brewery closed in 1860, and the tunnels were eventually abandoned. During Prohibition, they were pressed into service once again as a speakeasy. According to Craig Maness of American Legacy Tours, police raided the tunnels in 1923.

Abandoned once again, the tunnels were eventually filled in with dirt and brick and remained a tomb, sealed off and forgotten, for nearly a century. Today, the Linck Brewery Tunnels and their architecture and fermentation tanks remain a source of fascination for those fortunate enough to explore this underground world.

# 48 BOAR'S HEAD AND YULE LOG FESTIVAL

## What brings Beefeaters, torchbearers, and a wild boar's head to town each year?

The pageantry! The costumes! The sheer celebratory spectacle! The Boar's Head and Yule Log Festival is a Cincinnati holiday tradition that has its roots in an ancient pagan celebration dating back to the Middle Ages.

For more than seventy-five years, since 1939, the Episcopal Diocese of Southern Ohio has presented the festival at Christ Church Cathedral the weekend following Christmas. An evening performance takes place on Saturday, and two performances are held on Sunday. The best part? Tickets are free.

A gong sets everything in motion, with some 190 performers along with dozens of musicians and choir members adding their footfalls, voices, and colorful garb to the splendor and solemnity of the occasion: Beefeaters (traditional guardians of the king), a taper-bearing Yule Sprite, an angel, minstrel, knights and attendants, lords and ladies, shepherds and magi, and more. At its centerpiece is the boar's head, the conquered enemy, representing Christ's victory over evil.

Behind the scenes, another two hundred or so participants add their talent and toil to bring this lavish production, based

### BOAR'S HEAD AND YULE LOG FESTIVAL

**WHAT** Pig, pomp, and pageantry

**WHERE** Christ Church Cathedral, 318 E. Fourth St.

**COST** Free, ticket hotline 513-621-2627

**PRO TIP** Tickets are distributed on the second Saturday morning in December. They are first-come/first-served and limited to two tickets per person (must be eighteen and older).

cincinnaticathedral.com

(Left) *The annual Boar's Head event is Christ Church Cathedral's Christmas gift to the people of Cincinnati.* (Right) *It takes a village to stage the annual Boar's Head and Yule Log Festival. Photos courtesy of Christ Church Cathedral.*

on a legend dating to 1340s Oxford, England, and an incident at Queen's College, to the holiday stage inside the cathedral. It is believed that one of the festival's songs, "As Dew In Aprill," penned by an anonymous author in the thirteenth century, is likely the oldest carol showcased in the Boar's Head ceremony.

For all its pomp and circumstance and enormous cast, this "Miracle on Fourth Street," as the Boar's Head and Yule Log Festival has been called, opens each year without benefit of rehearsals. And every year it plays to a packed house.

---

See the Boar's Head Art Exhibit, *The Triumph of Good Over Evil*, with original props, photographs, and more in the church's south corridor, opened for the ticket giveaway and running through the final performance date.

# 49 CINCINNATI AVIATION HERITAGE MUSEUM

## Why is a "bathtub" hanging from the ceiling in the Lunken Airport terminal?

Remember when American Airlines routinely offered a champagne breakfast on its mid-morning flights? Chilled bubbly, fresh pineapple in shell, eggs Benedict, grilled red ripe tomato half, fresh berry muffins, and apple coffee cake accompanied by hot, freshly brewed coffee?

No?

See the evidence with your own eyes on a vintage American Airlines promotional card at the Cincinnati Aviation Heritage Museum, located inside the terminal at Lunken Airport.

The museum was founded in the late 1990s by a group of area aviation history buffs who eventually organized themselves as the Cincinnati Aviation Heritage Society. One piece of memorabilia, a large logo featuring the iconic AA Eagle that once hung behind every American Airlines ticket counter across the country, launched the museum.

Over time, additional pieces of American Airlines history have taken their place in the glass cases and on the walls and ceilings, including pilot caps and uniforms, pictures, posters and advertising pieces, and model airplanes. Lots of model airplanes, and for many well-known carriers: TWA, Comair,

---

Dig into a braunschweiger sandwich, smokehouse salad, or chicken wings at Sky Galley while watching jets take off and land. The restaurant, tucked into the Lunken Airport terminal, has a relaxed retro vibe.

*The Cincinnati Aviation Heritage Museum collects, restores and displays aviation artifacts relating to Ohio and the Cincinnati Tri-State. Photo courtesy of John Witt.*

## CINCINNATI AVIATION HERITAGE MUSEUM

**WHAT** Early aviation history

**WHERE** 262 Wilmer Ave., Second Floor, Room 26

**COST** Free

**PRO TIP** The museum has limited hours. If you see the open sign on the railing next to the yellow airplane hanging from above, head on up.

cahslunken.org

Republic, USAir, United Express, and TED, United's doomed idea for a low-cost airline.

One particularly interesting artifact is an Allegheny Airlines stewardess uniform, a cute little number with flounced skirt that harkens back to a time in the not-too-distant past when the girl had to fit the uniform, not the uniform sized for the flight attendant.

A visit to the museum yields some intriguing facts, like how the Aviation Corporation (AVCO) spawned Embry-Riddle Aeronautical University and American Airlines and why, according to Charlie Pyles, curator/treasurer of the Cincinnati Aviation Heritage Museum, general aviation is largely responsible for airline transport companies in the United States. This includes Aeronca, maker of the tiny Aeronca C-3 Flying Bathtub that hangs in the terminal lobby, which was built here, and Boeing, whose transports today are adorned with the huge GE (General Electric) turbine engines.

# 50 SHARON WOODS

**Why does the American Woodcock perform his sunset courting display flight at this park?**

Sharon Woods is the oldest of the Great Parks of Hamilton County, but she still has a lot of spring in her step.

## SHARON WOODS

**WHAT** Fossil forest

**WHERE** 11450 Lebanon Rd., Sharonville, OH

**COST** An annual Motor Vehicle Permit is required: $10/Hamilton County residents; $14/all others.

**PRO TIP** See samples of the various fossils found in Sharon Woods on the floor of the Nature Station. Each fossil was placed by hand as the surface was being poured.

greatparks.org

This 730-acre park is well known for its state-of-the-art Sharon Centre with nature exhibits, live wildlife, gift shop, and accessible two-story indoor Adventure Station; its miles of trails, including the 2.6-mile paved multi-purpose trail that circles Sharon Lake; the harbor with paddleboats, playground, and water-feature play area; and the Sharon Woods Golf Course, opened in 1938 by legendary golfer Bobby Jones.

What many don't realize is that because the park is bordered by industrial and residential areas, Sharon Woods has become an oasis of greenspace for a diverse variety of wildlife, including the American Woodcock. One of Sharon Woods's most unusual seasonal visitors, the woodcock is also a species most visitors have never seen or heard.

---

The Ohio Department of Natural Resources granted State Nature Preserve status to the twenty-one-acre Sharon Woods Gorge. It is the only state-recognized nature preserve in Cincinnati.

(Above) *Sharon Woods is a green haven for a variety of wildlife. Photo courtesy of Great Parks of Hamilton County.* (Right) *You never know what prehistoric creature you'll run into at Sharon Woods. Photo courtesy of John Witt.*

More charmingly called the timberdoodle in some circles, this plump, short-legged shorebird eschews lakeside living for a forest habitat where it can probe the ground for earthworms, slugs, and snails. Plumage allows it to camouflage itself amidst leaf litter, but in springtime, the male puts on a skydance at dusk for the females that is both dizzying and dazzling. And he gets so involved in his courting ritual that he is oblivious to human spectators.

Deep in the park but within a handful of miles to city shopping and dining is Sharon Woods Gorge, formed thousands of years ago by Ice Age glaciers bulldozing their way through the area. The steep-walled limestone and shale gorge is a mini-canyon measuring nearly one hundred feet deep in some places. Splashing through the gorge is Sharon Creek, a result of glacial erosion, its rocky shelves forming waterfalls throughout.

Because of the erosion, ancient fossils of creatures that lived in the Ordovician Sea that covered this portion of Ohio 450,000,000 years ago (brachiopods, trilobites, and graptolites, among them) can be found in the creek.

# 51 NATIONAL STEAMBOAT MONUMENT

## Where is the smoke from the smokestacks?

Twenty-four smokestacks and not a single curl of smoke.

They were made for Cincinnati's 2002 Tall Stacks, a once-frequent festival that gathered together replica and vintage steamboats from across the country at the Ohio River shoreline. Internationally famous Christopher Janney, an American composer/artist/architect known for his sound sculptures, designed the monument.

Rising from the Dan and Susan Pfau Whistle Grove on Cincinnati's Public Landing at Sawyer Point, the metal smokestacks are poised beneath a three-story, sixty-ton fiberglass red paddlewheel that soars forty feet above street level. It is an exact replica of the original one from the *American Queen*, the largest steamboat ever built and the very embodiment of Mark Twain's description of paddlewheel boats as tiered wedding cakes in all their frippery and finery.

The stacks once belched steam with abandon. Accompanied by the belting, blasting rhythms of the riverboat calliope, they not only showcased the importance of steam in the early days of riverboat travel but also recalled Cincinnati's mid-nineteenth century glory days during the riverboat era,

---

Journey through US history and nature aboard American Queen Steamboat Company's grand and gracious *American Queen* and luxurious all-suite *American Duchess*. Elegant voyages on the Mississippi and Ohio Rivers are offered, with a number of itineraries including Cincinnati.

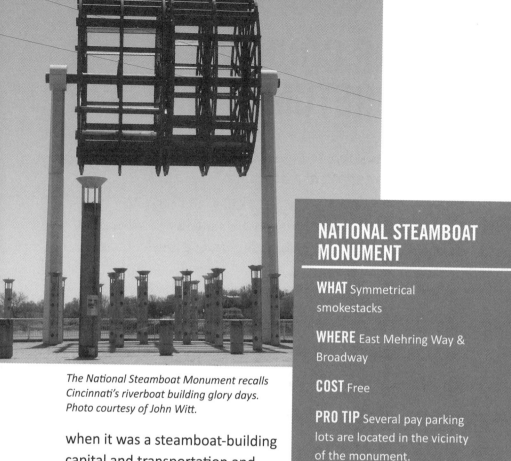

*The National Steamboat Monument recalls Cincinnati's riverboat building glory days. Photo courtesy of John Witt.*

## NATIONAL STEAMBOAT MONUMENT

**WHAT** Symmetrical smokestacks

**WHERE** East Mehring Way & Broadway

**COST** Free

**PRO TIP** Several pay parking lots are located in the vicinity of the monument.

cincinnatiusa.com

when it was a steamboat-building capital and transportation and commerce hub.

Alas, money and mechanical failure combined to render the stacks steamless; the calliope soundless; and the recordings of bluegrass and ragtime music, diary readings, and the general cacophony of voices raised in riverboat-related musings that once worked with a wave of the hand mute.

Still, visitors can wander along a pillared Steamboat Hall of Fame to learn about some famous (or infamous) riverboats of the era, like the circa 1863 *Sultana* that was carrying Union soldiers home at the close of the Civil War when it exploded on the Mississippi River in 1865, killing more than 1,700 people, and the circa 1867 *America* that collided the very next year with her sister, the *United States*, resulting in 74 casualties.

# 52 BOONE COUNTY ARBORETUM

**Where is it possible to enjoy the solace of greenspace and the noisy action of a ballgame?**

The Empress of China, a Cherokee Chief, and a devil's-walkingstick can all be spotted in the nation's first arboretum within an active recreation park setting, and they're not even among the rarest species.

The 121-acre Boone County Arboretum is not only one of the few places in the Greater Cincinnati area to learn about and explore such a unique arrangement of diverse plants, it is also an enormous trial site to identify which plants will or won't do well in the Cincinnati area. Not to mention a glorious garden for quiet walks and a hustle-bustle sports arena for watching kids play ball.

Three thousand six hundred trees and shrubs, plus a showy variety of annual and perennial flowers, reside within the

## BOONE COUNTY ARBORETUM

**WHAT** Sports fields in a garden

**WHERE** 9190 Camp Ernst Rd., Union, KY

**COST** Free

**PRO TIP** Because of the arboretum's unique layout with active recreation, it is best to visit during the week before mid-afternoon or earlier in the morning on weekends.

bcarboretum.org

Classes and programs for all ages are offered throughout the year, including Dig in the Dirt volunteer work days with lunch included, storytime/craft outings, educational-based workshops, and more.

*The Boone County Arboretum is a living museum providing a place for the appreciation and study of plants and the preservation of the natural environment. Photos courtesy of Kris Stone/Boone County Arboretum.*

arboretum's well-groomed borders, including such plant-world obscurities as needle palms, certain unusual conifers, rare oaks, and endangered poplars. The most unusual of these, the needle palm, a tropical beauty with deep green leaves, must be coddled and protected within a fenced area filled with leaves to help it survive winters this far north.

The plants meander around baseball and soccer fields and are grouped in collections: magnolia, crabapple, hydrangea, dogwood, evergreen holly, and more. Themed patches include a children's garden and rain, butterfly, and annual display gardens, among others. The two-plus miles of hiking/biking/walking trails are marked with names of tree species.

Other arboretum features include tennis courts, playground, and wildlife viewing area, plus a three-acre native Kentucky grassland surrounding a bird blind and overlooking a wetland area.

By arboretum standards, this one is young, having been dedicated less than twenty years ago in 1999. It is also tech-savvy, the country's first public arboretum to have its entire plant collection mapped with global positioning technology. Visitors can download a map and track every single plant in the arboretum if they are so inclined.

# 53 MITCHELL MEMORIAL FOREST

## Why are mountain bikers on the park loop?

Those who know about the 1,473-acre Mitchell Memorial Forest are avid fans who would prefer to keep this parcel of wild country overlooking the Great Miami River Valley to themselves. Those who discover it quickly fall in step and adapt the same mindset.

Off the beaten path and regularly missed by adventurers seeking out the larger Miami Whitewater Forest, Mitchell Memorial Forest feels hushed and remote. It is much smaller and more laid back than other Great Parks of Hamilton County and gets a lot less people traffic. If cozy is a word that can be used to describe a park, Mitchell is it, and that's what the locals love about it.

Its assets include a catch-and-release fishing pond ringed by a paved trail that is ideal for walking and running, the one-mile Wood Duck Trail, children's play structure and swings, restroom facilities, picnic areas, friendly rangers, and beautiful scenery, including an area named Tall Pines, where picnickers can claim a grill, chill, and watch deer nibble at brush in the field.

The big deal, though, is the eight-mile International Mountain Biking Association–approved Mountain Bike Trail, the first official such trail in Hamilton County. The trail is

---

The 4,438-acre Miami Whitewater Forest is the largest of the Great Parks of Hamilton County. Enjoy nature trails, horseback riding trails, nine-hole disc golf course, eleven-acre dog park, shelters, picnic areas, and more.

*Hamilton County's first official mountain bike trail is just over eight miles of fun and challenging trail features. Photo courtesy of Cecily Rose, courtesy of Great Parks of Hamilton County.*

## MITCHELL MEMORIAL FOREST

**WHAT** Mountain biking trails

**WHERE** 5401 Zion Rd., Miami Township, OH

**COST** An annual Motor Vehicle Permit is required: $10/Hamilton County residents; $14/all others

**PRO TIP** Portions of the Mountain Bike Trail can be hiked in sections, so there are lots of options for different, shorter hikes in the park.

greatparks.org

multiuse, so it accommodates walkers, runners, and hikers, too, particularly those looking for a long and vigorous workout: The trail is definitely challenging, with moderate and steep terrain, a few dips, and some rocky sections.

There are two loops, one for intermediate riders and one for advanced, each roughly four miles in length. One loop is a bit more technical because of the rocks, and both offer different snapshots of parkland scenery from flora to meadows to woods.

# 54 CINCINNATI DINNER TRAIN

## Where can you wear your forties fashions and fit right in?

A historic collection of rail cars transports dinner guests into the 1940s and the golden era of rail travel. Board a 1947 Budd-built New York Central dining car, an American Car & Foundry table car of the same vintage, or a car that once belonged to the Ringling Brothers and Barnum & Bailey Circus now known as the Oasis Tavern.

Brian Collins, co-owner of the Cincinnati Dinner Train, calls the beautifully restored railcars "land yachts."

"I feel like we're keeping the past alive," he said. "That was a special time, the 1930s through early 1950s, where you dressed up, had white linen tables and top-of-the-line dining as you traveled across the country."

The Cincinnati Dinner Train serves a slice of that history, one course at a time, over three courses, twenty-five miles and several hours, every

### CINCINNATI DINNER TRAIN

**WHAT** Travel by train into the 1940s

**WHERE** 2172 E. Seymour Ave.

**COST** $84.95 per person.

**PRO TIP** Turn onto Eagle off East Seymour (you'll see a sign for Green Sales) and take the first left into a parking lot. Check in at a tiny depot with a sign reading, "to the trains."

cincinnatirailway.com

See gardens and award-winning sculptures at Theodore M. Berry International Friendship Park, whose grand design was inspired from the simplicity of a child's friendship bracelet and is a tribute to world peace and unity.

(Above) *The Cincinnati Dinner Train serves up nostalgia as it gently rocks along two historic railroad lines, including Cincinnati's first railroad, toward the riverfront. Photo courtesy of John Witt.* (Left) *The New York Central dining car is ready to receive its dinner guests. Photo courtesy of Cincinnati Dinner Train.*

Saturday, March through November. The excursion rolls past a number of Cincinnati landmarks, including Lunken Airport, the Pioneer Memorial Cemetery, and the Theodore M. Berry International Friendship Park.

Guests are encouraged to get into the spirit of the outing and dress like it's 1949 (think shirtwaist dresses for the ladies, Zoot suits for gentlemen); in fact, Collins seeks out those dressed in period 1940s attire, choosing them for a tour of the locomotive cab when the train makes its riverfront stop.

Dinner begins with appetizers, moves on to entrées—including prime rib and salmon and accompanied by baked potato and veggies—and concludes with a homemade dessert. A full bar offers wine and cocktails. The Queen City Sisters, an a cappella women's trio, sing their swing from train car to train car and then on stage in the Oasis Tavern following dinner.

# 55 LLOYD LIBRARY AND MUSEUM

## Why is a still sitting in a Cincinnati library?

Among the many rare and beautifully illustrated tomes in the Lloyd Library's collection, one of the most precious and magnificent surely is the 1739 *A Curious Herbal*. A book of medicinal plants, it was a labor of love for artist Elizabeth Blackwell, who drew the illustrations, engraved the copper plates for printing, and hand-colored the printed images to raise funds to free her husband from debtor's prison.

It was an unappreciated gesture, to be sure. Not long after the husband, a derelict named Alexander Blackwell, was released from prison, he squandered the money and fled to Switzerland, where he was beheaded. Karma came through, and Elizabeth's book is today considered a canon in the field of botany.

Such are the tales and treasures to be uncovered at the Lloyd Library and Museum, downtown Cincinnati's home to scholars and leading experts in the fields of pharmacy, botany, ethnobotany (the intersection of anthropology and botany), chemistry, medicine, history, and botanical arts.

It all began in 1864 with the personal collection of research material acquired by brothers and pharmacists John Uri Lloyd (1849–1936), Nelson Ashley Lloyd (1851–1925), and Curtis Gates Lloyd (1859–1926), leaders in the field of Eclectic or natural medicine. The trio was part of a movement to form an

---

Coming to the Lloyd for research? Contact the librarians in advance; they can partner with you in your research and have resources, not immediately obvious, ready for your visit.

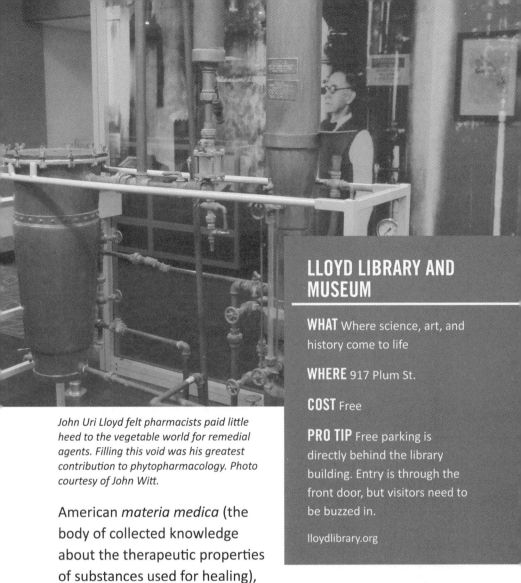

*John Uri Lloyd felt pharmacists paid little heed to the vegetable world for remedial agents. Filling this void was his greatest contribution to phytopharmacology. Photo courtesy of John Witt.*

## LLOYD LIBRARY AND MUSEUM

**WHAT** Where science, art, and history come to life

**WHERE** 917 Plum St.

**COST** Free

**PRO TIP** Free parking is directly behind the library building. Entry is through the front door, but visitors need to be buzzed in.

lloydlibrary.org

American *materia medica* (the body of collected knowledge about the therapeutic properties of substances used for healing), primarily using plant-based drugs indigenous to the United States.

Today, the collection contains some 250,000 items, more than 7,000 of which are rare and generally accessible only at the Lloyd. See travel bags and medicines from nineteenth-century pharmacists who made house calls; a Lloyd Cold Still used in the creation of medicines from natural plants; the Soxhlet extractor, used in the discovery of the anti-cancer drug Taxol; and the pharmaceutical invention Benadryl, an anti-allergen drug created by local Cincinnati scientist and philanthropist George Rieveschl Jr.

# 56 PEONY GARDENS

## Where can you enjoy lunch in a downtown garden setting?

No artist's brush can quite capture what Mother Nature herself presents in living color: the peony gardens in full bloom at the Taft Museum of Art.

### PEONY GARDENS

**WHAT** Lunch at the gardens

**WHERE** Taft Museum of Art, 316 Pike St.

**COST** Enjoying the Taft gardens is included with regular admission pricing. Some programs, including a Chamber Concert series, are free. Museum admission varies but it always free for active military, members, and children under eighteen.

**PRO TIP** The peonies are at their most spectacular in mid-May, offering incredible photo ops. It is estimated that there are around one thousand blooms.

taftmuseum.org

The flowers lining the walkway at the front of the house from Pike Street are a glorious explosion of color: ruby red, luscious pink, apricot, crimson, purple, salmon, and creamy white and ivory. They are joined by shade trees and shrubbery on a canvas of green lawn framed by black wrought-iron gates. It is a picture-perfect place to linger over a quiet lunch on one of Cincinnati's exquisite blue-sky days in spring and summer.

Although the peonies weren't planted until 1984, gardens have flourished at the Taft since the early- to mid-nineteenth century when it was a private home. The most extensive gardens were cultivated by Nicholas Longworth, who purchased the house in 1829 (price tag: $28,000) and lived in it until his death in 1863.

A prominent Cincinnati businessman, Longworth was a lawyer, abolitionist, and experimental horticulturist who succeeded in cultivating the Catawba grape on the banks of

*At least fifteen varieties of peonies are planted at the Taft Museum of Art. Photo courtesy of the Taft Museum of Art.*

the Ohio River. He was also an arts patron who commissioned the internationally famous African American artist Robert S. Duncanson to paint the landscape murals that may be seen in the museum.

British writer Harriet Martineau visited Longworth's "splendid house" on her two-year trip to the United States in 1834 to 1836. She wrote about the experience in her 1838 *Retrospect of Western Travel in Three Volumes*:

*"The proprietor has a passion for gardening, and his ruling taste seems likely to be a blessing to the city. He employs four gardeners, and toils in his grounds with his own hands. His garden is on a terrace which overlooks the canal, and the most parklike eminences form the background of the view. Between the garden and the hills extend his vineyard, from the produce of which he has succeeded in making twelve kinds of wine, some of which are highly praised by good judges. . . ."*

---

After a childhood spent in poverty in New Jersey, Nicholas Longworth came to Cincinnati in 1804, became an attorney, and amassed a fortune, thanks to his real estate investments. He is considered the Father of American Winemaking.

# 57 LOVELAND CASTLE

## Why was a castle built in Loveland?

This is the house that Sir Harry built. Except that it is actually a castle. And Harry D. Andrews was an American who happened to love everything medieval. A medic during World War I, Andrews was declared dead in 1918. Except that he wasn't. By the time the declaration was reversed, a very much alive Andrews learned he had lost his sweetheart. He decided to remain in Europe to do what he loved: explore castles.

When this can-do innovator returned to the home-front, he managed in 1927 to acquire a piece of land, by way of a newspaper subscription incentive, on the Little Miami River. Two years later, he began building what would become Chateau LaRoche ("rock castle"), combining the architectural styles of the English, German, and French castles he had seen in order to create his own masterpiece, a replica of a sixteenth-century medieval castle.

The footprint includes a kitchen, living room, dining room, bedroom, and office, as well as a balcony, dungeon, fighting deck, and much more. Among its features are four types of towers, domed ceiling, dry moat, stoop doors, even murder holes (those slits or spaces through which the keepers of the castle could fire or throw weapons, including arrows, rocks, scalding water, or tar). The castle was dedicated in 1930.

### LOVELAND CASTLE

**WHAT** European castle

**WHERE** 12025 Shore Dr., Loveland, OH

**COST** $5/person; free for kids five and under.

**PRO TIP** The castle is open weekends between October and March; daily, April through September. Annual Castle Days take place on the third Saturdays of April, May, June, July, and August.

lovelandcastle.com

(Above) *Chateau Laroche is the world headquarters and residence of the Knights of the Golden Trail. Photo courtesy of John Witt.* (Left) *The Loveland Castle in springtime. Photo courtesy of the Loveland Castle.*

Today, visitors can take a self-guided tour of the castle, its grounds and gardens, enjoy a picnic and the views, play a game of chess or checkers, even try to pick up on spectral activity as the castle is supposedly haunted. A collection of period weaponry is on display throughout the castle, and souvenirs are available for purchase.

---

Upon his death, Sir Harry willed the castle and grounds to the Knights of the Golden Trail (members of Andrews' Sunday School/Boy Scout troop). The knights guard the castle to this day.

# 58 MELAN ARCH BRIDGE

## Why do stone eagles roost at the bridge?

The first concrete arch span bridge constructed in Ohio is also the oldest reinforced concrete bridge in the United States. The Melan Arch Bridge was an engineering marvel when it was built over the main road in Eden Park, just beyond the Krohn Conservatory.

### MELAN ARCH BRIDGE

**WHAT** Curving stone bridge

**WHERE** Eden Park, Eden Park Dr.

**COST** Free

**PRO TIP** Walk along the sidewalk to the center of the bridge for a great photo op of Krohn Conservatory.

The year? Either 1894 or 1895. Sources contradict the year the bridge went up, but not the genius behind the arch system, developed in 1892 by Professor Joseph Melan of Austria-Hungary. It called for the use of stiff steel ribs or trusses encased in concrete to form the arch ring, and it was the steel that provided most of the strength required. The design was patented one year later in the United States.

Cincinnati's 117-foot-long structure with 70-foot span was designed and built by Austrian engineer Fritz von Empergen of the Melan Arch Construction Company. Four eagles carved of limestone flanking both entrances give it a distinctive look.

---

Krohn Conservatory was built in 1933, nearly forty years after the Melan Arch Bridge, when the Art Deco era was in full swing. It was renamed in 1937 for longtime Board of Park Commissioner Irwin M. Krohn.

(Above) *The Melan Arch Bridge in Eden Park.*
(Left) *The stone eagles embellishing the pillars at the Melan Arch Bridge came from the old Chamber of Commerce Building. Photos courtesy of John Witt.*

The eagles once perched at Cincinnati's old Chamber of Commerce building, a lavish, citadel-like structure that towered over the corner of Fourth and Vine, but it burned down in 1911, and the birds alit on the stacked stone pedestals in Eden Park.

The symmetry of the overall design evokes an old-fashioned mantelshelf and is wholly charming. The bridge frames views of the tree-lined road winding into the distance. A pedestrian walkway on the top of the bridge connects Eden Park's Memorial Groves to the Donald Spencer Overlook, which presents a breathtaking cityscape view. Spencer was a founding member of the Friends of Cincinnati Parks. Also, here is the Ohio River Monument, dedicated by President Herbert Hoover in 1929 to commemorate the canalization of the river for year-round water transport.

# 59 CINCINNATI OBSERVATORY

## How did the "Birthplace of American Astronomy" wind up in Cincinnati?

A National Historic Landmark, the Cincinnati Observatory is considered to be the "Birthplace of American Astronomy." As the oldest public observatory in the country, a fact that many visitors find surprising, this remarkable stargazing center, perched at the end of a cul-de-sac in a residential neighborhood of prim Victorian homes, is an important part of Cincinnati history as well as the history of the United States.

"We house the oldest public telescope still in use for viewing in this hemisphere in our Mitchel scope," said Anna Hehman, director of development. "The scope was purchased in Bavaria by our founder, Ormsby MacKnight Mitchel, and saw first light on April 14, 1845."

What Mitchel saw in that historic first peek through the telescope is documented. He described seeing the moon, "her mountain heights, her rocky precipices and her dells." Jupiter was chronicled as a "globe of surpassing splendor." Of the Saturnian system, he wrote, "the mind over whelmed in wonder and astonishment."

The observatory is actually housed in two buildings. The main building was constructed in 1873, with the dome added nearly twenty years later in 1895, and housing the sixteen-inch Clark telescope. It was made in 1904 in Cambridgeport,

---

Cincinnati architect Samuel Hannaford designed the observatory. Other buildings in his portfolio include Cincinnati's City Hall, Music Hall, and the Cincinnatian Hotel.

*Restored to its original beauty, the Observatory is a fully functioning nineteenth century observatory used daily by the public and amateur astronomers. Photo courtesy of the Cincinnati Observatory.*

## CINCINNATI OBSERVATORY

**WHAT** Stargazing with historic telescope

**WHERE** 3489 Observatory Pl.

**COST** $5, with proceeds benefiting the observatory's programs.

**PRO TIP** The Cincinnati Observatory hosts weekday tours at 1, 2, and 3 p.m., Monday through Friday. Tours include both observatory buildings and two main telescopes.

cincinnatiobservatory.org

Massachusetts, by Alvan Clark and Sons. That same year, the smaller of the two buildings went up. This building features two domes and houses the eleven-inch Merz and Mahler telescope (the scope Hehman referred to as the Mitchel scope).

Because the buildings have been around so long, and possibly due to their purpose, many visitors expect them to be haunted. Experts have evaluated the buildings for supernatural presence and, with apologies to ghost hunters everywhere, have never found a single shred of evidence. Still, the many stargazing classes and programs open to the public more than make up for the lack of spectral activity.

# 60 MERCANTILE LIBRARY

## Where can you read for free in a private-club setting?

"What a place to be in is an old library!"—Charles Lamb

Yes, it's a membership-based library, but anyone can slip inside the stately Mercantile Library Building in downtown Cincinnati, take the elevator to the eleventh floor, enter beneath a fitting Charles Lamb quote to a polished enclave, and rummage among the stacks for a favorite volume of poetry to while away the day. And it's free.

The Mercantile Library has been around for a long time, since 1835 when a group of forty-five merchants founded it as a means for networking and self-education. It holds an astounding collection of eighty-thousand-plus books, including contemporary fiction, non-fiction, history, travel, and more. It also hosts a thriving program of literary-themed events.

The library keeps things perpetually interesting with a roster of erudite lecturers and speakers who discourse on a wide array of subjects (politics, art, literature, science, religion, and more). In fact, a historical marker next to the front door noting past prominent speakers will blow you away: Herman Melville, Harriet Beecher Stowe, William M. Thackeray, Ralph Waldo Emerson.

The atmosphere in the library is one of hushed relaxation, the tone set by the *Goddess of Silence* with finger shushing at her lips. Leather sofas and chairs are arrayed on oriental rugs atop wood floors that gleam warmly with a patina

---

The Mercantile Library, one of only two dozen surviving membership libraries in the United States, is in the extraordinary position of having a ten-thousand-year prepaid lease, renewable in perpetuity. You've got time to get there.

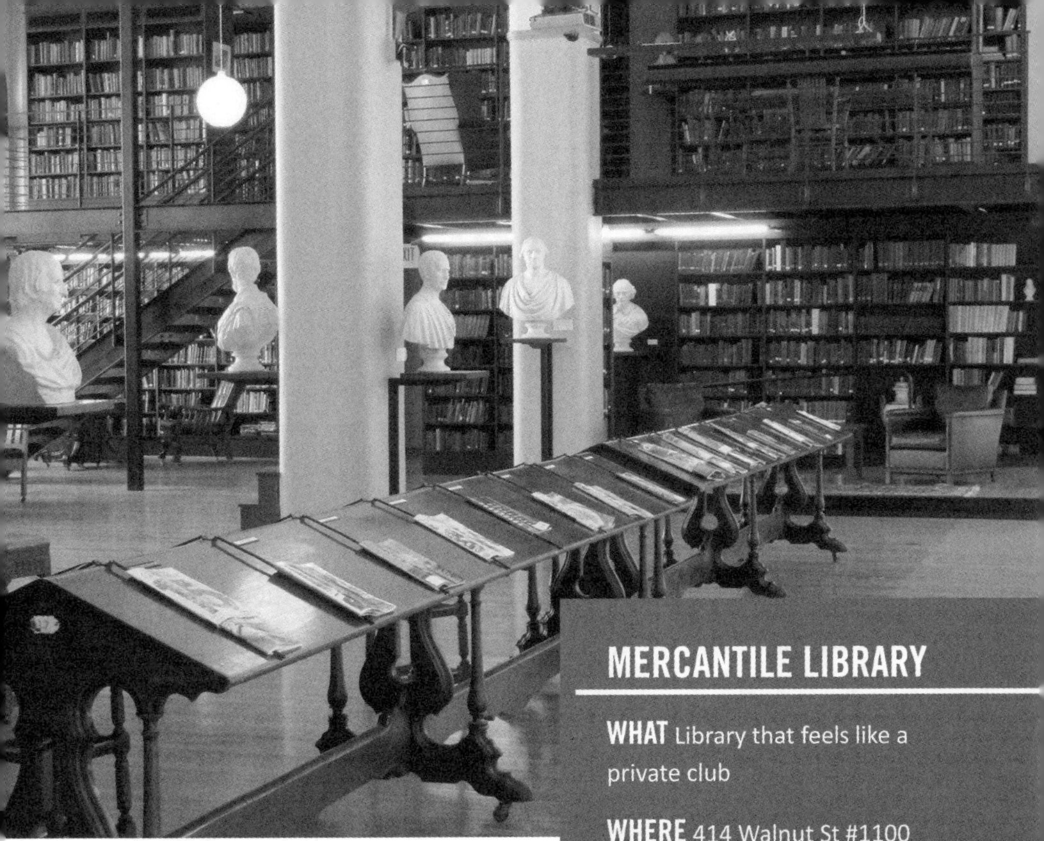

A calming oasis in the heart of the city, the Mercantile Library offers extremely pleasant environs for enjoying a good book. Photo courtesy of John Witt.

## MERCANTILE LIBRARY

**WHAT** Library that feels like a private club

**WHERE** 414 Walnut St #1100

**COST** Free

**PRO TIP** Use of the library's reading room is for members only (checking out books, using Wi-Fi, working, etc.). Members may also take yoga classes for free.

mercantilelibrary.com

earned from decades of footfalls of both renowned and not-quite-so-renowned visitors. Arched windows look out over downtown hustle-bustle. Portraits of significant personages and statuary, including busts, lend a professorial air, but mainly, the library is inviting and beautiful, a quiet respite from the workaday world outside.

The Mercantile Library presents a lively schedule of Literary Evenings that typically feature nationally recognized authors, poets, and journalists. Signature events include the Words and Music Lecture, Hearth and Home Lecture, and Modern Novel Lecture.

# 61 RAILWAY MUSEUM OF GREATER CINCINNATI

### Why is this graveyard full of old trains?

A 1912 post office on wheels with an interior equipped to sort thousands of pieces of mail. A 1928 car that once transported theatrical scenery to stages across the country. A 1939 Pullman sleeping car that stepped up as a staff car for the US Army Medical Corps.

Pass through the gates of the Latonia Rail Yard to learn about Cincinnati's railroading history at this rugged train graveyard, with its collection of railroad stock and signal displays.

The volunteer-run Railway Museum of Greater Cincinnati opens on Saturdays for visitors to explore the historic train cars on self-guided tours. Maps and descriptions of the railcars are highlighted in a pamphlet available at the welcome booth. The museum is an active restoration site, but volunteers will talk trains, offer guided tours if possible, and share the lineage of each piece of equipment.

One car has an exceptionally interesting story. The Pullman-built circa 1914 Jovita shows the sleeping accommodations aboard trains a century ago. Talk about lack of personal space.

Picture the scene from the 1954 holiday classic, *White Christmas*, when Bob Wallace (Bing Crosby) hoists Betty

#### RAILWAY MUSEUM OF GREATER CINCINNATI

**WHAT** Train cars and tours

**WHERE** 315 West Southern Ave., Covington, KY

**COST** $4/adults; $2/ages ten and under.

**PRO TIP** The museum is open only on Saturdays, May through October, or by special arrangements. See www.facebook.com/cincirailmuseum for updates.

cincirailmuseum.org

(Above) *The volunteer-run Railway Museum of Greater Cincinnati preserves Cincinnati railway history.* (Right) *Some lucky visitors get to tour the Pullman-built circa 1914 Jovita car at the Railway Museum of Greater Cincinnati. Photos courtesy of John Witt.*

Haynes (Rosemary Clooney) down from her top berth, or the one from 1959's *Some Like It Hot*, in which Marilyn Monroe, Jack Lemmon, and at least a dozen members of the all-girl band crowd into the top berth for a tipple. The only thing separating you from the passenger one bed over was a thin piece of fabric.

The Jovita is the last of this particular series of cars that has not been modified. Its authenticity is probably why it had a starring role in the movies *Lost in Yonkers* and *Eight Men Out*.

A grassy park with shaded tables adjacent to the train museum offers a nice place to extend your visit with a picnic. Pick up deli sandwiches and snacks at Latonia Market around the corner.

---

A few blocks from the train museum, Tim's Train & Hobbies stocks more than three thousand items for model railroading, rocketry, car, plane, and ship hobbyists. Look for the train mural on the side of the building.

# 62 BAKER HUNT ART & CULTURAL CENTER

## How did Covington inherit a house for a cultural hub?

The woman who gifted the home that would become the Baker Hunt Art & Cultural Center, a hub for learning, cultural enrichment, and artistic expression, got the idea from a relative (an Adams of the presidential Adamses, no less) who had donated a home to the community of Portsmouth, New Hampshire.

Despite losing her daughter, Katie, to meningitis on her fifteenth birthday, her mother two years later, her husband three years after that, and her father the following year, Margaretta Baker Hunt remained community-focused and an avid supporter of education and the arts. With no heirs, she established the Baker Hunt Foundation in 1922. It's mission? "The promotion of the Education, Art, Science, Psychic Research and Religion in the vicinity of Covington, Kentucky."

Wait! Psychic research? At one point in the home's history, and lasting for thirty years, Margaretta used her deceased daughter's room for psychic research and demonstration. This was conducted by Cincinnati medium Laura C. Cooper Pruden, famous for her seances and slate-writing. Also called "spirit-writing," it was the appearance of writing on a blank slate, purportedly through the intervention of the spirits.

---

Visit Baker Hunt's Heritage Gardens with unusual trees and outdoor artwork and the Baker Hunt Family Museum with three rooms of items owned by the Baker-Hunt Family, including the quilt made for Katie's birthday, which she never got to use.

*The Baker Hunt Art & Cultural Center sits on a shady street in Covington. Photo courtesy of John Witt.*

## THE BAKER HUNT ART & CULTURAL CENTER

**WHAT** Hands-on workshops

**WHERE** 620 Greenup St., Covington, KY

**COST** Free for garden, museum, and some events; fees for classes and workshops.

**PRO TIP** Baker Hunt partners with Tony Award-winning Playhouse in the Park and its "Off the Hill Productions" to present free, family friendly live theatre at Baker Hunt.

bakerhunt.org

These days, visitors to Baker Hunt Art & Cultural Center find a rich roster of classes for all skill levels: watercolor and oil painting, cartooning, manga drawing, language, ballet, tai chi, guitar, pottery, photography, and everything in between. Each season brings new sessions, and all classes are taught by professionally trained teachers. More than 3,500 students from the tri-state area annually attend classes.

Having spent more than ninety-five years involved in creating art and preserving history and culture, the Baker Hunt campus remains pleasant and peaceful, and it is one of the places you can sit and enjoy nature and still see the Cincinnati skyline. It is a lovely backdrop for concerts, twilight garden events, children's plays, and at least two resident ghosts.

# 63 MOTHERHOUSE GROUNDS OF THE SISTERS OF CHARITY OF CINCINNATI

## Why is a maze in the cemetery?

Follow the walking path from the shaded grotto on the eastern lawn of the Motherhouse Grounds with its statue of Our Lady of the Springs and a kneeling Saint Bernadette Soubirous, past St. Joseph with the Christ Child statue and the Peace Pole, beyond the Mother Margaret George Statue to the Mt. St. Joseph Cemetery and its Labyrinth.

Getting there is like embarking on a pilgrimage, but that is the point in this place that naturally provokes contemplation.

Pilgrims should clear their minds and step into the circular maze, winding their way to its center as they meditate, repeat a mantra, or reflect on a specific question or intention. Modeled after the labyrinth found on the floor of Chartres Cathedral in France dating from 1221, it is here for purposeful meditation in one of the most inspirational settings in the Cincinnati area.

The Motherhouse Grounds roll out along the heavily forested banks of the Ohio River with glimpses of the water showing through breaks in the foliage. It is shaded and calming, with birds chirping and trilling, squirrels scampering about, and wind rustling through the leaves.

---

Part of the global Peace Pole Project, the Motherhouse Peace Pole features eight languages, five human, and three representations (paw prints, leaves, celestial bodies) that represent facets of Sisters of Charity ministries.

*The grotto at The Motherhouse Grounds of the Sisters of Charity of Cincinnati is a place of quiet beauty. Photo courtesy of John Witt.*

## MOTHERHOUSE GROUNDS OF THE SISTERS OF CHARITY OF CINCINNATI

**WHAT** Walkable wonderland

**WHERE** Delhi and Bender Rds.

**COST** Free

**PRO TIP** Stop by or contact the front desk (513-347-5300) to let the Sisters know you would like to tour the grounds.

srcharitycinti.org

The Sisters of Charity of Cincinnati first arrived in the area in 1829. They were a feisty lot that founded schools, staffed orphanages, and worked as nurses during the Civil War. In 1880, they built the Mount St. Joseph Motherhouse on this land and, in 1920, founded the College of Mount St. Joseph.

A significant section of the grounds is given over to the cemetery, the final resting place of more than 1,700 Sisters, with the first grave created in 1883 for Mother Regina Mattingly. Also resting here are those Sisters who served in the Civil War and the Congregation's original seven founders.

A self-guided walking tour includes nine places to see on the Motherhouse Grounds.

# 64 ST. MARY'S PARK

## Why is a park dedicated to Mary nicknamed the Fountain Square of Northern Kentucky?

A peaceful park built directly across from the Cathedral Basilica of the Assumption provides the perfect place not only to ruminate over the gargoyles and chimeras leering down from this architectural marvel, but also to see two different interpretations of Mary on the cathedral's façade.

A relief narrates the Assumption of the Blessed Virgin into heaven and sits in an arch over the cathedral's main entrance. Between the central doors is a statue of the Madonna and Child. Both were carved by Cincinnati sculptor Clement Barnhorn and are fitting companion pieces to a third portrayal of Mary, this one a nine-foot-tall bronze statue holding the infant Jesus, the centerpiece of Covington's new St. Mary's Park.

With graceful lines and gentle visage, this sculpture rests atop an octagonal-shaped fountain in the midst of Cathedral Square, adjacent to the Diocesan

### ST. MARY'S PARK

**WHAT** City sanctuary

**WHERE** Corner of Martin Luther King Blvd. and Madison Ave., Covington, KY

**COST** Free

**PRO TIP** St. Mary's Park closes at 4 p.m.

saintmaryspark.org

Beautifully landscaped, St. Mary's Park fulfills a manifold purpose as urban oasis, pilgrimage site, and community gathering space. Plans call for a second statue, Our Lady of Knock, to join St. Mary.

(Above) *Part of Cathedral Square, St. Mary's Park is as urban oasis open to the public.* (Right) *St. Mary's Park complements the art of the Cathedral Basilica of the Assumption with its own inspirational sculpture. Photos courtesy of John Witt.*

Curia Building and across from the cathedral. The figure is ringed by benches, and the park is enclosed by black fencing.

Classically designed, the David Frech sculpture depicts an exquisitely beautiful Mary as a young mother clutching her baby to her chest. At once dignified and approachable, she is shown with sleeves pushed up, chin ever-so-slightly inclined toward her son and eyes nearly closed, perhaps in contemplation of what the future holds.

At the park's 2016 dedication, the sculptor said the water in the fountain is meant to convey the mysteries of life. With the statue rising majestically above it from its four-foot stone pedestal, one can't help being reminded of the Tyler Davidson Fountain (or the *Genus of Water*) that bedecks Cincinnati's Fountain Square and was dedicated 145 years before the fountain in St. Mary's Park was unveiled. Not surprisingly, the new statue has been nicknamed the "Fountain Square of Northern Kentucky."

# 65 MUSEUM OF ANTHROPOLOGY

### How did ceremonial masks and totem poles get here?

Complex and colorful bead art and yarn paintings of the Huichol peoples, inhabitants of the Sierra Madre Mountains of Mexico, have symbols of fire, earth, and healing woven into motifs of deities and serpents.

A performance and ceremonial button blanket, sometimes called a totem pole on cloth, represents a very personal belonging among peoples of the northwest coast. Decorated with abalone shells, a sign of wealth, the blankets are highly regarded for their animal symbolism and embellishments and lead to an understanding that wealth can be shared among families.

Faces of the Hmong, Dao, and Tai cultures of Southeast Asia—a colorful, ancient way

#### MUSEUM OF ANTHROPOLOGY

**WHAT** Array of artifacts

**WHERE** Northern Kentucky University, Landrum Academic Center, Room 200, Highland Heights, KY

**COST** Free.

**PRO TIP** Museum hours are by appointment. Note the museum is closed during summer months.

anthropologymuseum@nku.edu

In addition to the museum, visitors can attend Northern Kentucky University Theatre productions. Its highly regarded Theatre and Dance Department stages several shows annually and also produces the biennial Y.E.S. Festival of New Plays.

*Intricate bead work are art forms created by the Huichol peoples of Mexico. Photo courtesy of John Witt.*

of life marked by beautiful and intricate clothing, particularly hats—create a form of unspoken communication that expresses a specific cultural heritage.

Tucked away on the second floor inside Landrum Academic Center on the campus of Northern Kentucky University (NKU), the Museum of Anthropology offers visitors a chance to learn about other peoples' lifestyles, behaviors, and interests.

Dr. James Hopgood, a former head of the Department of Anthropology at NKU who began teaching here in 1973, was founder and director of the museum, which opened in 1976. To build the collections, Hopgood encouraged faculty members to buy artifacts on their fieldwork expeditions and bring them back to display. They acquired collections from around the world: the Philippines, Southeast Asia, Mesoamerica, Africa, and the United States.

The 1,500-plus objects include ethnographic as well as archeological materials from local digs and excavations; they tell the stories of the cultural communities that make these objects. But the museum also provides training opportunities to undergraduates, teaching hands-on skills to students who help create special exhibits from collection pieces at NKU and other venues, including public libraries.

The museum is a small but significant treasure trove that showcases carved masks, beaded garments, blankets, jewelry, sculptures of figurines and other items, pottery, tools, and more.

# 66 OLD LUDLOW INCINERATOR

**Why are scary ruins on a park trail?**

If the ruins of Ludlow's old trash incinerator aren't haunted, the spectral realm has seriously missed an opportunity.

Forsaken and forgotten by all but hapless wanderers who stumble upon it and hikers and bikers who purposely brave the aptly named Incinerator Trail, the brick shell of the structure and its stack sit on land in Ludlow, covered in graffiti that includes a sinister smiley face with leering mouth and big red eyes.

Built in the 1940s, the incinerator was decommissioned in the 1960s and has been languishing away for half a century while awaiting its fate.

The site is accessed from the Ludlow ballfield parking lot off Sleepy Hollow Road, just past the Old Montague entrance to Devou Park (coming from Dixie Highway), and actually has a directional kiosk located nearby.

Plans to create a shelter and rest area in the vicinity of the incinerator are on the distant horizon, but a number of steps need to be taken first, including determining how much of the structure can be salvaged. Because the site is also considered a brownfield (previously developed land where the possibility of contamination may exist), environmental remediation will be required for redevelopment.

---

While there are no spirits at the old incinerator, there are elsewhere in Ludlow; specifically, at Second Sight Spirits, an artisan distillery crafting small-batch rum and moonshine.

*What's left of the Old Ludlow Incinerator lends a creepy air to the trail named for it. Photo courtesy of John Witt.*

For now, the shell and stack may be seen "as is" on the 1.2-mile trail named for the business that formerly occupied the site. The trail itself is narrow and spools out along switchbacks, moderately challenging with its incline and retaining the creepy atmosphere that hangs over the incinerator ruins.

## OLD LUDLOW INCINERATOR

**WHAT** Eerie remains

**WHERE** Devou Park, 440 Deverill St., Ludlow, KY

**COST** Free

**PRO TIP** Beyond the old incinerator are more than eight miles of well-used mountain bike and hiking trails in Devou Park.

covingtonky.gov/visitors/parks/devou-park

# 67 PYRAMID HILL SCULPTURE PARK & MUSEUM

**Why is a giant scribble drawing erupting from a field in the countryside?**

> **PYRAMID HILL SCULPTURE PARK & MUSEUM**
>
> **WHAT** Giant art park
>
> **WHERE** 1763 Hamilton Cleves Rd., Hamilton, OH
>
> **COST** Adults: $8/adults; $3/ children ages six-twelve; free, children ages five and under.
>
> **PRO TIP** Tour Pyramid Hill by Art Cart, a golf cart, rented first-come first-served, that lets you drive right up to the sculptures for an up-close view.
>
> pyramidhill.org

Emerging round each bend in the road, monumental sculptures rise from the rolling topography against a seasonal canvas that changes with Mother Nature's whims.

The lyrical *Abracadabra,* by Alexander Liberman, is as mesmerizing as a three-dimensional scribble drawing. The massive, twelve-ton bronze *Euclid's Cross* by Michael Dunbar reflects the artist's machine-age sensibility. George Sugarman's *Cincinnati Story*, inspired by the Ohio River, splashes toward the surrounding trees.

The sculptures are among some sixty modern and contemporary works by world-renowned artists adding drama, color, energy, and splendor to Pyramid Hill Sculpture Park & Museum, an outdoor museum set picturesquely amidst rolling hills and overlooking the Miami River Valley.

It is a legacy to Cincinnati made possible by the late visionary and philanthropist Harry T. Wilks, a lawyer who once admitted he knew nothing about sculpture. Wilks created a public foundation to protect the land so it could never be

*Pyramid Hill Sculpture Park is one of the largest parks of its kind in the country. Photo courtesy of John Witt.*

subdivided or developed.

The large-scale sculptures are showcased on 335 acres, one of the few sculpture parks of its size in the country. The land is enhanced with meadows, ponds, hiking trails, gardens, native plants and habitats, and even the vestiges of a long-ago settler habitation with its circa 1820s Pioneer House. The overall setting clamors for attention, and bonus: You can touch the sculptures and also bring your dog (as long as it is leashed).

As modern as the outdoor sculptures are, the onsite Ancient Sculpture Museum reaches all the way back to 1550 B.C. with its six dozen pieces from Greek, Roman, Etruscan, Syrian, and Egyptian eras, including a sarcophagus of Ankh-Takalot. The Museum Gallery hosts changing exhibitions of local, regional, and national artists, and the Founder's Library presents a visual history of the park.

Wilks's former private residence, the underground Pyramid House, has been renovated as an events venue available for rentals.

---

Pyramid Hill's annual Holiday Lights on the Hill features a two-mile roundtrip drive through thousands of lights and illuminated holiday vignettes. It takes place mid-November through end of the year and is open daily, including holidays.

# 68 SYMPHONY HOTEL & RESTAURANT

## Where are Beethoven, bourbon, and barramundi combined for a showstopping encore?

"If music be the food of love, play on."

Shakespeare would have loved the Symphony Hotel & Restaurant, a restored 1871 townhome sumptuously transformed into a boutique hotel in downtown Cincinnati's OTR neighborhood, where it elegantly melds a European sensibility with a laidback American vibe.

Maestro-inspired guestrooms are a natural tie-in to Music Hall, located just across the street. Each of the nine individually decorated rooms are named and themed for the top names of the composing world: Mozart, Malher, Beethoven, Bach, Rachmaninoff, Brahms, Beech, Schubert, and Copeland. Six of the rooms are tucked into the original mansion; three are in the newer section.

The two buildings are connected by an intimate bar and tasting room tailor-made for fireside bourbon tastings; outside, they share a courtyard perfect for summertime wine sipping. Classical and comfortable, the Symphony is all about good music and food.

The restaurant serves contemporary New American cuisine that changes seasonally but always focuses on healthy, partnered with a strong emphasis on locally sourced

### SYMPHONY HOTEL

**WHAT** Out-of-the-way watering hole

**WHERE** 210 W. 14th St.

**COST** See website.

**PRO TIP** On Thursdays the Symphony offers complimentary valet parking. A fee is charged for valet parking on Friday and Saturday. For Sunday Brunch, try Washington Park Garage or street parking.

symphonyhotel.com

*The Symphony Hotel is an urban hideaway serving dinner Thursday through Saturday, Sunday brunch and live jazz music. Photo courtesy of John Witt.*

ingredients: wild fish, free-range chicken, grass-fed rib-eye. Don't look for a deep fryer in this award-winning kitchen. Everything is made from scratch, including rich, bite-size desserts that headline quality over quantity to keep taste buds and waistlines both happy and in harmony.

The Symphony serves dinner on Thursday, Friday, and Saturday nights and offers a Sunday Brunch, all served on linen-draped tables amidst stunning Italianate architecture and vintage furnishings. Mimosas, lattes, and ambrosia? At the morning, coffee, and tea bars. For those holding tickets to a showing at Music Hall, the hotel's five-course menu is an exquisite prelude sans the fear of missing the opening act. For hotel guests, breakfast is served daily.

Those in the know like to gather in the hotel's bar and lounge for Kentucky bourbon and seasonally inspired craft cocktails as well as live jazz music, performed Thursday, Friday, and Saturday nights.

---

Besides being close to Music Hall, the Symphony Hotel is cattycorner to concert-friendly Washington Park and within an easy stroll of the Art Deco–style Ensemble Theatre and mega open-air Findlay Market.

# 69 WOLFF PLANETARIUM

## Where can you sit with the stars and seventeen of your closest friends?

The oldest public planetarium west of the Allegheny Mountains may be the most exclusive ticketed event in town. That's because the intimate space of the Wolff Planetarium inside the Trailside Nature Center in Burnet Woods can seat only a cozy eighteen beneath its twelve-foot diameter dome.

Erected in 1939 as a natural history museum, the building inspired by Frank Lloyd Wright's Fallingwater included a small dome, but it was never intended to be a planetarium. The projector came later, and museum staff would remove display cases to set up for planetarium shows during the winter months.

Today, live interactive shows are generally held on the third Friday evening of the month (although the schedule changes from time to time due to other program commitments.) You won't find pre-recorded shows here, but an ad-libbed adventure through the stars, with the inspiration for each show drawn from the seasonal constellations visible at certain times of the year.

Along with being the oldest, Wolff Planetarium may also be the most low-tech of planetariums, its equipment a Spitz model A-1 planetarium projector that was purchased in the 1950s. Audience participation is a must. (Who better to supply the sound effects?)

Michael George, the naturalist whose domain is the Trailside Nature Center, sets the simulated sky to what attendees can see from their own backyard on the particular evening of their visit. Stories spun hail from Greek and Roman mythology, but Native American and African folk tales also get their due. George gives it his all, peppering the show with diverse myths, obscure facts about the stars, even "bad star jokes."

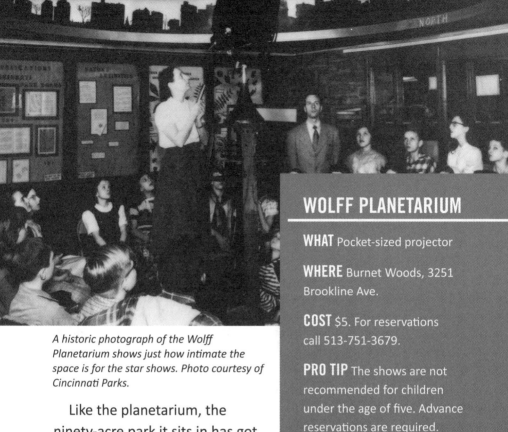

## WOLFF PLANETARIUM

**WHAT** Pocket-sized projector

**WHERE** Burnet Woods, 3251 Brookline Ave.

**COST** $5. For reservations call 513-751-3679.

**PRO TIP** The shows are not recommended for children under the age of five. Advance reservations are required.

cincinnatiparks.com/central/burnet-woods

*A historic photograph of the Wolff Planetarium shows just how intimate the space is for the star shows. Photo courtesy of Cincinnati Parks.*

Like the planetarium, the ninety-acre park it sits in has got some years on it but remains spry with lots of activities. One of Cincinnati's oldest parks, Burnet Woods has a fishing lake, nature library, crafts room, and exhibits. Outdoors are playgrounds, shelters and picnic areas, a historic bandstand, and a disc golf course.

---

The Audubon Society named Burnet Woods an Important Birding Area (IBA). Because of its mix of mature deciduous woodland, scrub areas, treed lawn, and pond, it is an "urban stopover for energetic restoration and successful continued migration" of woodland birds.

# 70 PLAY LIBRARY

## Why does this library shelve Serpent Pirate Ships, Monster Trucks and Chuckle Balls?

Board games, building sets, puzzles, role-playing games, electronics, playsets, musical instruments, and more. Here is a titanic toy chest whose sole mission is all play/all day with an ever-growing inventory that includes more than one thousand toys and games, even seasonal outdoor equipment. Croquet, anyone?

Standing on a corner in Cincinnati's OTR neighborhood, its interior perked up with quirky illustrations by local artists, the Play Library is unique among traditional lending libraries in that instead of fiction, "playtrons" check out fun. Big fun, with diversions for all ages and interests: Ring Toss, Poker, Zany Zoo, Gooey Louie, Pop the Pig, 3Doodler and Spiral Doodles, several versions of Scrabble, Barbie Glam Pool, a Build Your Own Volcano. Whiz kids can also make new toys from old and assorted toy parts.

Play with the toys and games onsite in the Play Library's bright, splashy space with irresistible swings for seats, or check them out for playtime and game nights at home. Toys and games are a mix of the latest, greatest, and hottest stuff in town and high-quality donated items. (And germaphobes fear not: When toys are checked back in, they don't return to the shelves until thoroughly sanitized.)

### PLAY LIBRARY

**WHAT** Fun and games on loan

**WHERE** 1517 Elm St.

**COST** Free to play onsite. Memberships start at $15/month.

**PRO TIP** The Liberty/Elm St. Streetcar stop is one stop north of Washington Park. Area street parking is free; parking lots are within two to three blocks.

playlibrary.org

(Above) *The Play Library is tucked in a beautiful building in downtown Cincinnati. Photo courtesy of* John Witt. (Right) *Grab some fun at the Play Library. Photo courtesy of the Play Library.*

A non-profit business that survives on monetary donations and memberships, the Play Library uses play to bring families and communities closer, lets kids try before the parents buy, and helps keep once-loved playthings out of landfills.

Play Library is an out of the (toy) box destination for birthdays and other occasions. Monthly games nights and other play events are hosted regularly. Held less frequently, Toy Hospital invites kids to bring in toys that need to be repaired and lovies that need to be restuffed. All "patients" leave with a toy wrapped in gauze and a Dum Dum Lollipop.

---

Play Library is home to Cincinnati's first Toy History Museum. Learn about the Easy Bake Oven, Magic-8 Ball, Uno, and other iconic toys that got their start in Cincinnati, home of Kenner from 1946 to 2000.

# 71 THORNTON TRIANGLE'S TECUMSEH STATUE

## Why is an unnamed statue known as Tecumseh?

Cincinnati's smallest public park is so miniscule that passersby could easily miss it while driving through the streets of Saylor Park.

Measuring a mere one tenth of an acre, this tiny parcel known as Thornton Triangle sits at the intersection of Gracely Drive and Thornton Avenue. What makes it remarkable is a zinc composition statue depicting a cloaked Tecumseh, looking majestic with bow and arrow as he peers into the distance from atop his cast-iron pedestal.

Could be the Shawnee Native American chief, born in Ohio and killed during the War of 1812, is wondering why the sculpture's plaque reads simply: "Erected in memory of J. Fitzhugh Thornton by his wife Eliza M. Thornton, January 15, 1912."

There is no mention of Tecumseh, possibly because the sculpture was never actually intended to be Tecumseh, but representative of an eastern Woodlands Native American. One of nine such (remaining) statues in the United States, it is based on a nineteenth-century design by New York City woodcarver Samuel Anderson Robb (1851–1928), whose niche was carving ventriloquist puppets, circus wagons, and

### THORNTON TRIANGLE'S TECUMSEH STATUE

**WHAT** Woodlands Native American sculpture

**WHERE** 6600 Gracely Dr., Saylor Park, OH

**COST** Free

**PRO TIP** The statue has survived the Great Flood of 1937, the tornado of 1974, being struck twice by a car, and being sold off, found, restored, and reinstalled.

cincinnatiparks.com

*#53 Indian Chief is more familiarly known as Tecumseh. Photo courtesy of John Witt.*

traditional cigar store Indians.

From Robb, the design went to William Demuth (1835–1911), a penniless immigrant from Germany who went on to establish the William Demuth Company in New York and turn it into possibly the country's largest pipe import, wholesale, and manufacturing business.

In addition to pipes, Demuth specialized in cigar store figures and other carved objects. In 1872, the statue was cast in metal, copyrighted, and the design sold as #53 Indian Chief. One year later, it appeared in the 1873 catalog of J.L. Mott Iron Works.

Besides #53 Indian Chief, it is known by several names, including the J. Fitzhugh Thornton Memorial and the Fernbank Indian (a nod to Saylor Park's former village name). Tecumseh seems to be the name that sticks.

---

On April 3, 1974, Saylor Park was hit by a devastating F5 tornado during Super Outbreak (what the National Weather Service called the "the worst tornado outbreak in US history"), April 3 and 4 of that year.

# 72 PRESERVATION LAB

## What's hidden behind the closed doors of this library?

Once a year, the doors to this chamber of secrets are opened and the public is invited in to see how the sausage is made, or remade, in this case.

The Preservation Lab at the University of Cincinnati Libraries annually hosts an afternoon Open House, and anyone can follow the signs to its third-floor location and wander from station to station to see rare and precious books that have been coaxed back to health by a crack team trained in more than two dozen ways to repair and restore historic works. Also on display are the conservation tools and techniques used to perform what are in some cases medical miracles.

The Open House takes place in late April during Preservation Week, an initiative of the Association for Library Collections & Technical Services, a division of the American Library Association.

### PRESERVATION LAB

**WHAT** Conserved collections

**WHERE** University of Cincinnati Libraries, 300 Langsam, 2911 Woodside Dr.

**COST** Open house is free.

**PRO TIP** Park in the Woodside Drive lot off Burnet Ave., take the steps up to the campus quad, and enter the library at the fourth floor. The Preservation Lab is one flight down.

libraries.uc.edu
blog.thepreservationlab.org

---

Words never tasted so good! The University of Cincinnati Libraries annually celebrates the International Edible Books Festival on or about April 1. The free-admission festival is open to the public.

*Learn about preservation and conservation for your own book collections during the Preservation Lab's annual Open House. Photo courtesy of John Witt.*

The behind-the-scenes peek includes "don't touch" items and enough "touch" pieces to satisfy itchy fingers. You might handle a model of a Nag Hammadi codex (also known as the Gnostic Gospels) that dates from the fourth century, paired with a photograph pre-restoration.

A walk through the evolution of the book form, from cuneiform to contemporary artist's book, gives an appreciation for the lab's "doctors," whose bags of tricks include skillsets of researchers, artists, engineers, chemists, and photographers. During Open House, they answer questions, provide preservation tips, discuss the history of rescued collection materials, and oversee the hot stamper where visitors crank out souvenir bookmarks.

This venue is the first collaborative lab in the country, serving the University of Cincinnati Libraries and the Public Library of Cincinnati and Hamilton County. The conservation techs don't work on private collections; rather, they work on special collections, like a cache of teaching assignments and letters written by William Howard Taft during his years as dean (1896–1900) of the University of Cincinnati Law Department.

# 73 WITHROW NATURE PRESERVE

### Why is this preserve best for communing with nature?

One of Cincinnati's least-developed parks is the perfect place to lose yourself for an hour or an afternoon, the quiet broken only by scampering wildlife.

Located in Anderson Township, the 270-acre Withrow Nature Preserve is a serene sanctuary with mature forest and prairie areas, an overlook offering a splendid glimpse of the Ohio River, wooded areas with wildflowers that are especially alluring in springtime, and open fields that put on a summertime show of butterflies flittering about milkweeds and songbirds twittering and warbling.

This year-round idyll was established through the efforts of several individuals and entities, including the Nature Conservancy, to preserve the area's habitat and wildlife. Adelaide Withrow donated her home, named Highwood, and its surrounding land to Great Parks of Hamilton County in 1980.

The park remains a pristine refuge with a diverse landscape populated by nature's mixed bag of denizens: bluebirds and goldfinches, daisies and purple coneflowers, black cherry and pawpaw trees.

---

Withrow Nature Preserve offers a hundred-seat outdoor wedding venue with gazebo that shows off Mother Nature's handiwork at its lushly forested best. Reservations include climate-controlled bride and groom changing rooms at the Highwood Lodge.

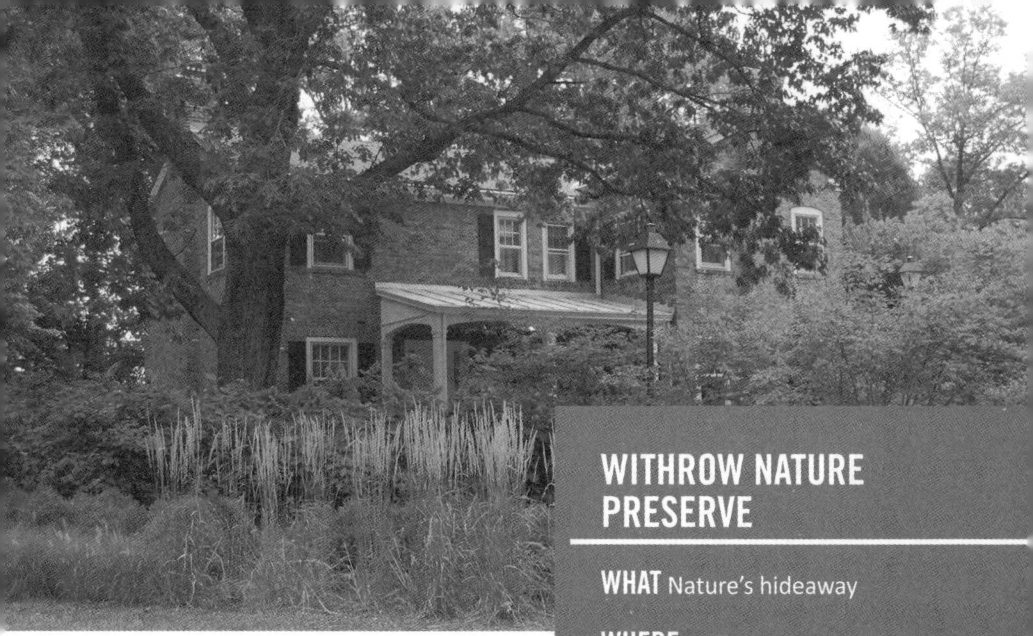

*This Great Parks provides an idyll for hikers. Photo courtesy of Great Parks of Hamilton County.*

## WITHROW NATURE PRESERVE

**WHAT** Nature's hideaway

**WHERE** 7075 Five Mile Rd., Anderson Township, OH

**COST** An annual Motor Vehicle Permit is required: $10/ Hamilton County residents; $14/all others

**PRO TIP** The 1.7-mile Trout Lily Trail has a more diverse and concentrated area of native spring wildflowers than any other Great Parks of Hamilton County park.

greatparks.org

The preserve is deep, well-shaded, and cooling with mighty oaks and hickories, maples and elms. Carpeting the grounds are such springtime beauties as large flowered trillium, Dutchman's breeches, squirrel corn, Virginia bluebells, wild ginger, bloodroot, and hepatica, looking dainty with its pink, white, and purple blossoms.

Wide and winding paths and mostly gentle inclines make for a lazy meander along the Trout Lily Trail, named for one of the flowers native to the preserve, the woodland-loving trout lilies with their yellow bell flowers. The bench seating at the overlook beckons hikers to forego their workout, sit down, and drink in the river view.

Early risers to the park are treated to nature awakening: white-tail deer grazing, wily gray squirrels frisking overhead in the trees, strutting wild turkeys claiming their turf, hungry owls pursuing their last nightly meal.

# 74 PRISONERS LAKE

## Why is a Greater Cincinnati lake named for convicts?

Surrounded by hardwoods and evergreen trees, Devou Park's Prisoners Lake is a placid spot to drop a line for rainbow trout, largemouth bass, and sunfish. Not much is heard over the plink of bait hitting the water or bees buzzing among the flora.

About one hundred years ago, the sound level at the lake was at a much higher decibel: an ear-splitting, rock crushing level. That's because the land now occupied by the lake was a stone quarry.

In 1916, a collective lightbulb went off over the heads of members of the Covington City Commission. Why not conserve city coffers by putting prisoners from the local jail to work at the quarry? At the time, Covington was forking over the not-insignificant sum of $18,000 a year for crushed stone to feed the city's ongoing need for building and repairing city streets.

Rock-crushing jailbirds would save the city $10,000 a year.

Equipment was purchased, inmates were dispatched from the Covington Jail, and work commenced at the quarry.

Almost immediately, a slight wrinkle in the plan revealed itself: The quarry proved to be an excellent place to escape, and many prisoners did exactly that during the first few years of the operation.

---

A Youth Fishing Derby, held by the Covington Parks and Recreation Department, takes place at Prisoners Lake annually on National Kids to Parks Day, with ages five to fifteen competing for prizes.

*Fish swim where jailbirds once walked at Prisoners Lake in Devou Park. Photo courtesy of John Witt.*

## PRISONERS LAKE

**WHAT** Neighborhood fishing hole

**WHERE** Devou Park, Prisoners Lake Dr.

**COST** Fishing license required.

**PRO TIP** Dedicated parking is available alongside the road across the street from the lake. A Got-A-Go! Unit is near the lake entrance for those heeding nature's call.

covingtonky.gov

Less than ten years later, by 1924, the quarry was gone and a large lake filled the space, taking its name from those who once labored on the site.

Today, Prisoners Lake covers nearly four acres and is part of the Fishing in Neighborhoods (FiNS) program. While boating isn't permitted, fishing is, and the lake has historically hosted fishing derbies. A statewide fishing license is required for anglers, and a trout permit is needed in order to keep trout per the Kentucky Department of Fish & Wildlife Resources.

# 75 OHIO BOOK STORE

**Where can you sell old books, get the family bible repaired, and see a page right out of history from 1499?**

If paradise was lined with paper, this would be it: The Ohio Book Store is a heavenly kingdom of 300,000 books. On five floors. Books from all genres and on every subject imaginable. Shelves and shelves of used and rare books, even some new ones, published by the Ohio Book Store, that showcase Cincinnati history.

To walk into this downtown domain with its green awning and terra cotta front exterior is to enter a wonderland of the written word.

Allow yourself to get lost in the stacks of fiction, representing the store's largest category of books. Following closely behind are books on religion, philosophy, and art. The books are a huge part of the business, but the shop also buys used books and offers an appraisal service with an expert in used and rare books, restoration services, and inhouse book binding.

## OHIO BOOK STORE

**WHAT** Book lover's paradise

**WHERE** 726 Main St.

**COST** Free to browse and bargains abound.

**PRO TIP** The folks who work at Ohio Book Store are always happy to help guide you or search for anything you may be looking for. Just ask.

ohiobookstore.net

---

Custom binding is a specialty at Ohio Book Store. A wide variety of cover materials are available, including leather, imitation leather, linen, and library buckram, all offered in a range of colors.

(Above) *Ohio Book Store has a constantly changing inventory of books spread over five floors.* (Left) *James Boswell was considered to be one of the world's greatest diarists. A collection of his private papers is valued at $2,000. Photos courtesy of John Witt.*

The bindery was opened in 1984, and Ohio Book Store has repaired and restored every type of book ever published, from tomes dating back to the 1400s and well-worn family bibles to dogeared cookbooks and popular fiction of a much more recent vintage. Shop owner Jim Fallon, who began working at Ohio Book Store in 1957 at age thirteen, recalls the bindery began with Ticket No. 1, followed by 28,690 tickets and counting. Each ticket could be one volume or more.

In business since 1940, the book store fills up the floors of a historic 1916 Gothic Revival-style building. Browsers might pick up the new *Cincinnati and the Civil War 1865* by Robert Wimberg, the last in a five-volume series on the Civil War, or something hundreds of years old, like Daniel Drake's *Picture of Cincinnati*, published in 1815.

Not for sale is a page from *Klonische Chronik* that dates back to 1499; what a kick to see this remnant from a religious history volume more than five hundred years old.

# 76 RIVERSIDE DRIVE STATUE TOUR

**How come the guy reading on the bench never turns the page of his book?**

A sketchpad, bridge plans, a textbook. Pilot wheel, walking stick, weapon. Each tells a story about a historical figure from the pages of Kentucky's past that intersects with Cincinnati history at the Ohio River. The items belong to seven bronze statues located along Riverside Drive in Covington's Historic Licking Riverside neighborhood.

Beginning at the foot of the Roebling Bridge, stroll down Riverside Drive, a beautiful street lined with stately mansions, toward the confluence of the Licking River with the Ohio to meet these celebrities from previous centuries.

First up is the civil engineer who bridged the waterway between Kentucky and Ohio at this particular bend in the river. Prussia-born John Augustus Roebling was the pioneer of the suspension bridge. The bridge he built here (started in 1858 and completed in 1866) was the prototype for the more well-known Brooklyn Bridge, a glory hog spanning the East River from Brooklyn to Manhattan Island in New York City.

Roebling's Cincinnati bridge was originally called the Covington-Cincinnati Bridge, later renamed the John A. Roebling Bridge, and known as the singing bridge by locals.

---

Author of *The American Boys Handy Book* and illustrator of several books for Mark Twain, Daniel Carter Beard is best known for his role with Boy Scouts of America. His house and statue are at 322 East Third Street, a private residence.

*The Riverside Drive Statue Tour is like a Hollywood Walk of Fame only with celebrities, including John Augustus Roebling and Captain Mary B. Greene, straight from the pages of history and the backdrop the Ohio River and Cincinnati skyline. Photo courtesy of John Witt.*

## RIVERSIDE DRIVE STATUE TOUR

**WHAT** Historic figures

**WHERE** Riverside Drive, Covington, KY

**COST** Free

**PRO TIP** Bring coffee or pack a lunch and sit a spell with James Bradley, who represents the Underground Railroad Movement on the tour.

nkyarttours.com/riverside-drive-statue-tour

Other tour notables are legendary frontiersman and soldier Simon Kenton, who famously saved the life of his pal, Daniel Boone, in 1777; the first licensed riverboat captain along the Ohio and Mississippi Rivers, Captain Mary B. Greene, who bought the *Delta Queen* paddlewheel boat following World War II; Little Turtle, chief of the Miami, who received a ceremonial sword from George Washington; and American ornithologist, naturalist, and painter John James Audubon, whose *Birds of America* became the standard-bearer of wildlife illustration. (Audubon was once briefly jailed for bankruptcy.)

Seated on the park bench overlooking the river? That is James Bradley, an enslaved man who bought his freedom in 1833, enrolled in Cincinnati's Lane Seminary, and, in 1834, was a featured speaker at the famous antislavery debates that took place at the Cincinnati seminary.

# 77 PAINTED LADIES

## THE PAINTED LADIES

**WHAT** Victorian row

**WHERE** Columbia Tusculum Historic District, off Columbia Parkway at Delta Ave.

**COST** Free

**PRO TIP** The streets are tight in Columbia-Tusculum and parking is practically non-existent. It is best to park wherever you can find a spot and walk.

columbiatusculum.org

### Why does this neighborhood feel (and look) a bit like San Francisco?

Blue trimmed with fuchsia and lime green. Red accented in yellow and gold. Orange set off by purple and pink. If it looks like a rainbow exploded over a clutch of homes stepping up the hills in a neighborhood perched high above the Ohio River, it is because you've found your way to the Painted Ladies.

The term refers to any set of Victorian or Edwardian houses that uses three or more colors to show off the architectural detailing of their design. These wildly popular architectural styles spanned the mid-nineteenth century, beginning with the reign of Queen Victoria through and beyond that of King Edward VII (1901–1910).

Hear the term and it inevitably calls to mind one of the most famous collections of this particular type of home. That is, San Francisco's row of color-saturated Victorian houses known as the Seven Sisters (or Postcard Row), located on Steiner Street across from Alamo Square.

But Cincinnati has its own Painted Ladies, thank you very much. About three dozen of them, including the "Tusculum Eight," are located in its oldest neighborhood, founded in 1788 and now known as the Columbia Tusculum Historic District.

The splashy exteriors help show off the intricate architectural appointments of the homes: ornate cutouts

The term, "Painted Ladies," was first coined in 1978. It was used in the title of the book *Painted Ladies—San Francisco's Resplendent Victorians*, by Elizabeth Pomada and Michael Larsen, to describe the famous row of houses.

*One of the eight Painted Ladies on Tusculum Avenue in Cincinnati's beautiful Columbia Tusculum Historic District. Photo courtesy of John Witt.*

and spindles, turrets, bay windows, gingerbread, porches with fretwork. Small but lushly planted front gardens and fanciful fencing add even more color and interest.

The houses didn't start out wearing these coats of many colors. This was the result of the so-called colorist movement of the 1970s that had its roots in the psychedelic 1960s. What began as unabashed self-expression transformed entire blocks of houses into today's color-wheel wonders that are truly a sight to see.

Not surprisingly, many of the homes in the Columbia Tusculum Historic District are listed on the National Register of Historic Places.

# 78 ROTARY GROVE MEMORIAL

## Why are Romanesque ruins in Devou Park?

Stroll the walking paths at Devou Park in Covington and you may spy a bridal party gathered for wedding photographs within a stand of trees, up the hill and across the road from the Band Shell.

With its stacked stone columns constructed of native fieldstone, topped with a pergola canopy, and sitting amidst towering trees, the Rotary Grove Memorial evokes ancient Roman ruins, but this shrine is of a much more recent vintage.

The Covington Rotary Club created the grove in 1932 by planting trees in memory of its deceased members and as a way to enhance the beauty of Devou Park. The club had been established in 1920, granted its charter by what is now known as Rotary International, the service organization founded originally in Chicago in 1905 with the goal of improving the quality of life in the group's home and world communities.

The dedication ceremony at Devou Park, held that same year on June 7, was planned in connection with the organization's George Washington Bicentennial program, which included planting a tree in honor of President Washington and carrying the idea into a memorial to honor deceased members.

Over the next decades, additional trees have been planted, along with shrubs, ground cover, and flowering perennials

### ROTARY GROVE MEMORIAL

**WHAT** Not-so-ancient ruins

**WHERE** Devou Park, Corner of Rotary Lane and Bandshell Blvd., Covington, KY

**COST** Free

**PRO TIP** The memorial is an ideal spot for meditating, reading, or remembering a loved one. A picnic table is located in the grove.

dreespavilion.com

(Above) *Rotary Grove is a scenic backdrop for wedding photos and a pleasant place for quiet enjoyment of Devou Park.* (Left) *Creating the Rotary Grove was a beautification project to benefit Devou Park. Photos courtesy of John Witt.*

to create this well-shaded garden room. A staircase and brick-paved walkway lead to the grove, which steps down to a plaza and a monument, inscribed with the name of each member memorialized.

---

Currently the site of the Kentucky Symphony Orchestra's annual Summer Series at Devou Park, the Band Shell was completed in 1939, a Great Depression–era Works Progress Administration (WPA) project.

# 79 SECRET GARDEN TOUR

**Why would more than one hundred people file onto a bus without a clue where they're going?**

Ah, the intrigue.

You board a bus, destination unknown, placing your fate in the hands of what likely is a complete stranger. The doors slam shut, and the bus goes trundling down the road. Your family has no idea where you are, and you have no clue where you're going.

It is truly a magical mystery tour, and about one hundred madcaps throw caution to the wind each time the tour is announced and fork over a hundred dollars apiece to be part of this day-long cliffhanger.

The payoff? Entrée into some of the grandest and most lavishly and intricately designed gardens in Greater Cincinnati. Adding to the hush-hush nature of these outings, the bus heads to a different neighborhood for each tour. Past excursions have ushered the lucky ticket holders into edens in Indian Hill, Hyde Park, Glendale and Wyoming, OTR and Newport, Kentucky, Columbia-Tusculum and Western Hills.

Presented by the Cincinnati Horticultural Society (CHS), the tour showcases neighborhoods and gardens selected by members who brainstorm about where to find the most spectacular gardens and go into the field, so to speak, to scout locations and knock on doors. The goal? Signing on gardens both grand and unique, generally inaccessible to the public.

---

The Secret Garden Tour is limited to one hundred participants and always sells out. It historically takes place the second Saturday of June, but it is not scheduled every year.

*See some of Cincinnati's most magnificent gardens on the Secret Garden Tour. Photo courtesy of Cincinnati Horticultural Society.*

## SECRET GARDEN TOUR

**WHAT** Grand gardens

**WHERE** The point of origin changes each year. Participants are advised once they are confirmed on the tour.

**COST** $100 (includes transportation/tour/continental breakfast/lunch).

**PRO TIP** Learn when a Secret Garden Tour is scheduled by visiting the CHS website and subscribing to its mailing list.

cincinnatihorticulturalsociety.com

Tour participants meet for a continental breakfast at the appointed location, then they are whisked off to four gardens. A break for lunch sometimes includes a speaker, after which the tour continues to three or four additional gardens. It is full-on, full-day touring to see Mother Nature at her show best.

The Cincinnati Horticultural Society was established in 1989. One of its objectives was to found the Cincinnati Flower Show. The organization also offers events and programs throughout the year, including a Gardener Recognition program, which was the impetus for creating the Secret Garden Tour.

# 80 WOODLAND MOUND

## Where is the mound of Woodland Mound?

Local experts and park officials say there is an ancient Indian burial ground somewhere within the one thousand-plus acres comprising Woodland Mound, unmarked and hidden for protection.

### WOODLAND MOUND

**WHAT** Water and wetland fun

**WHERE** 8250 Old Kellogg Rd.

**COST** An annual Motor Vehicle Permit is required: $10/Hamilton County residents; $14/all others.

**PRO TIP** American toads make their yearly spring migration to the manmade pond in the butterfly garden adjacent to Seasongood Nature Center. Want to hear the male toads serenade the females? Head there the first week or so of April after a good rain.

greatparks.org

You won't see it hiking along the miles of trails crisscrossing the park, or while executing scooby shots and hyzer flips on the eighteen-hole disc golf course. You will probably forget the search once inside the three-story Seasongood Nature Center, with its wildlife exhibits, interactive and sensory activities, children's nature programs, and gift shop.

Step outside to one of two observation decks and you will be treated to sweeping views of the Ohio River Valley. Because of its eastside location, Woodland Mound completely owns the view, sharing what is possibly the best panorama of any park in Cincinnati.

A little-known lure of this park, which opened in 1930, is the boat launch ramp, open pending river conditions. Boaters can bring their own boats, purchase daily and annual boat launch permits at the visitor center, and take off on an adventure on the Ohio River.

*Don't go to Woodland Mound expecting to see Woodland Mound. Photo courtesy of Great Parks of Hamilton County.*

Much more high-profile is Parky's Wetland Adventure, a splash park that feels more like a waterpark and with water baby enticements, including a sixteen-foot tree with two slides and water shooting, bubbling, spraying, and spurting from the ground and assorted woodland creatures like frogs, turtles, and heron. Located at the Breezy Point Pavilion, Parky's also features a dry playground and picnic areas where families can carouse the day away.

---

A secret will be revealed in 2030: As part of the official opening ceremonies of Woodland Mound, park commissioners installed a time capsule at Breezy Point Pavilion. It will be opened at the Centennial Celebration.

# 81 ST. MARY'S CATHEDRAL BASILICA OF THE ASSUMPTION

## Where can you replicate the experience of visiting the great cathedrals of Europe?

Crouching gargoyles, flying buttresses, French Gothic architecture. One almost expects to see the Hunchback lumbering up to the tower to ring the bells. That's because St. Mary's Cathedral Basilica of the Assumption in Covington is patterned after the medieval Notre-Dame Cathedral in Paris, France—the exterior façade, at least. The interior, an astonishing 180 feet in length and 81 feet in height, is modeled after a medieval abbey church in Paris, the Cathedral Basilica of Saint Denis.

The story of the cathedral goes back to the late nineteenth century, considered the heyday of church building. It was the dream of the Most Reverend Camillus Paul Maes, the third Bishop of the Diocese of Covington, the oldest Catholic parish in Northern Kentucky. Building began in 1894 and continued until 1901. In 1954, Pope Pius XII elevated the cathedral, which was incomplete and remains so today, to the rank of minor basilica, which

### ST. MARY'S CATHEDRAL BASILICA OF THE ASSUMPTION

**WHAT** A piece of Paris in Covington

**WHERE** 1101 Madison Ave., Covington, KY

**COST** Free; small fee applies for docent-guided tours for groups of ten or more.

**PRO TIP** Self-guided and docent-guided tours are available. Docent-guided tours are often given after Sunday's 10 a.m. mass.

covcathedral.com

*St. Mary's Cathedral Basilica of the Assumption was designed by artist and architect Leon Coquard, known as "America's Cathedral-Builder, and underwritten in part by a sizable donation from two local distillers. Photo courtesy of John Witt.*

confers ecclesiastical privileges and status.

Today, St. Mary's Cathedral Basilica of the Assumption is one of eighty-four designated minor basilicas in the United States. Majestic and almost achingly beautiful, this Bishop's Church is a treasure trove of art: murals by Covington artist Frank Duveneck; gilded wood carvings from Cologne, Germany; Italian Carrera marble altars and statuary; eighty-two stained glass windows, including the world's largest church stained glass window.

The Schwab pipe organ is one of only two playable Schwab organs in existence. Built in 1859 by Matthias Schwab, it was saved from the wrecking ball that decimated Covington's St. Joseph's Church, restored and rededicated in the early 1970s, the inspiration for the creation in 1975 of an annual Cathedral Concert Series.

And then there are the gargoyles and their equally grotesque brethren, chimeras. Exact copies of the fifty-six figures atop Notre-Dame Cathedral, these hideous creatures roost along the roofline, their purpose unknown. Are they there as decoration, to ward off evil, or for some sinister intent?

---

The Cathedral Concert Series presents classical instrumental and choral concerts of sacred music on Sundays, monthly October through May. Concerts are free (freewill offering accepted) and open to the public. See the schedule at cathedralconcertseries.org.

# 82 PIONEER MEMORIAL CEMETERY

## Where is a settlement that predates Cincinnati memorialized?

A mere month before Losantiville, later renamed Cincinnati, was founded, Major Benjamin Stites (1734–1804) of New Jersey established the settlement of Columbia on November 18, 1788. It was the first in Hamilton County and second in the "Old Northwest."

Accompanying this Revolutionary War soldier was fellow founder and soldier Ephraim Kibbey (1756–1809). Both frontiersmen were the Ohio equivalent of the legendary Daniel Boone. Also part of the expedition: twenty-five other like-minded adventurers, including four women and two boys.

Stites's settlement is the site of the oldest cemetery in Hamilton County, located where the circa 1790 Columbia Baptist Church once stood. The cemetery, barely more

### PIONEER MEMORIAL CEMETERY

**WHAT** First settlement site

**WHERE** 333 Wilmer Ave.

**COST** Free

**PRO TIP** A parking lot is located immediately off of Wilmer Ave. at the bottom of the cemetery grounds.

A memorial marker honors American Revolution Sgt. William Brown (possibly buried here), who served under Colonel Alexander Hamilton and is one of three soldiers awarded the Badge of Military Merit, predecessor of the Purple Heart.

*A colonial garden has been planted at the Pioneer Memorial Cemetery as a memorial to a former Park Board supervising horticulturalist. Photo courtesy of John Witt.*

than two acres, is all that remains to remind people that a tiny band of pioneers once forged a community on this land now part of the Columbia Tusculum Historic District and overlooking Lunken Airport.

Called the Pioneer Memorial Cemetery or Columbia Baptist Church Cemetery, it is on the National Register of Historic Places and maintained by Cincinnati Parks. Among the weathered tombstones is a memorial marker to Major Stites and markers of many Stites family members, including Phebe Stites. The daughter of Captain Hezekiah Stites, young Phebe died at five months old in 1797. Her tombstone is the oldest now existing in the cemetery.

Peaceful, well-shaded and maintained, the cemetery occupies its own little world along Wilmer Avenue. Some tombstones are scattered on the rise beyond the parking lot, but most are found on the grounds at the top of several sets of steps. A monument recalling "the First Boat-load," erected in 1879, is also here.

At the bottom of the stairs and adjacent to a stone footpath is a colonial garden, planted as a memorial to Frederick L. Payne. A supervising horticulturalist for the Park Board, Payne undertook a restoration project from 1967 to 1971, which resulted in a permanent record of the history of the cemetery and its occupants.

# 83 WINOLD REISS INDUSTRIAL MURALS

## Why is a wall of murals running the length of Central Avenue?

For four decades, they cast a long shadow in the train concourse of Cincinnati's Union Terminal, a glittering backdrop to the hustle-bustle of passengers scurrying to catch trains or get home.

From 1973 until 2007, when the shuttering of Terminals 1 and 2 hid them away from public view, they towered over passengers from all over the world checking in and passing through the Cincinnati International Airport.

From both locations, they beckoned passersby to slow down, take notice, and tune in, compelling them to see their stories, richly told in thousands of brilliantly colorful glass mosaic tiles that seamed together a tapestry of the factory worker's life in early twentieth century Cincinnati. But each time, their story was cut short when their canvas was razed.

German Art Deco artist Winold Reiss created these massive twenty-foot by twenty-foot masterpieces in 1933 during the Great Depression to pay tribute to the Everyman toiling over his labor as he works to build a better Cincinnati: cutting soap, milling tools, butchering hogs, building airplanes, making steel.

---

When Winold Reiss came to Cincinnati in 1931 for the murals, he stayed at a French Art Deco–style hotel, what is now the Hilton Cincinnati Netherland Plaza. It is home to Orchids at Palm Court, Ohio's only AAA Five Diamond Restaurant.

*See a factory worker pouring molten iron into a mold at the Winold Reiss Industrial Murals. Photo courtesy of John Witt.*

## WINOLD REISS INDUSTRIAL MURALS

**WHAT** Worker murals

**WHERE** Duke Energy Convention Center, Central Ave. between Fifth and Sixth Sts.

**COST** Free

**PRO TIP** Learn more about the artist and the murals in Gretchen Garner's Winold Reiss and the Cincinnati Union Terminal: Fanfare for the Common Man.

Companies featured in the murals include several still operating in Cincinnati, including Procter & Gamble, US Playing Card, and E. Kahn's & Sons, now known simply as Kahn's.

In 2016, nine of the works came back to Cincinnati to take up residence in their new home at the Duke Energy Convention Center. Given a nearly million-dollar spit shine and encased in state-of-the-art protective glass, the eight-inch-thick, eight-ton murals are free for all the world, at least those fortunate enough to put themselves downtown on Central Avenue, to see and enjoy.

# 84 MUSHROOM HOUSE

**How did fungus sprout in one of Cincinnati's most prestigious and classically beautiful communities?**

Looking as proud as the fungus version of a peacock is the so-called Mushroom House, a thorn (or perhaps, more accurately, a toadstool) among the architectural roses that characterize the stately manses typifying Cincinnati's Hyde Park neighborhood.

The Mushroom House was the vision of Terry Brown, a former architecture professor at both the University of Cincinnati and Miami of Ohio. Years of study and architectural know-how went into each and every design element of the morel-like masterpiece, from the cedar shakes Brown taught himself to cut to articulate his concept to the window shapes designed to be both ocular and anthropomorphic. These include one suggesting the unblinking eyes of a great owl and another the shades of one seriously cool hepcat.

Funky and fanciful, this head-turner sprouting from its hilly corner counted the architectural ideals of Frank Lloyd Wright and Bruce Goff, as well as Native American traditions, among its sources of inspiration. Teamwork went into its construction, with trusted craftsmen-collaborators carrying out Brown's vision in the house's windows, furnishings, and other appointments.

---

Terry Brown was no slouch in the building design department. With undergrad and master's degrees in architecture, he was a Fulbright Scholar in Vienna, Austria, and held positions at high-profile architecture firms in New York and Philadelphia.

*The Mushroom House is an architectural anomaly on the Cincinnati housing landscape. Photo courtesy of John Witt.*

## MUSHROOM HOUSE

**WHAT** Architectural toadstool

**WHERE** 3331 Erie/3518 Tarpis Ave.

**COST** Free

**PRO TIP** Photo ops are a challenge as the house sits on a heavily traveled main drag and a mesh of cables crisscrosses the front of the home.

By Hyde Park standards, the one-bedroom, one-bath geometrically contorted cottage is fairly small at 1,200-plus square feet, but its sometimes almost-shaggy showstopper of an exterior, perked up with a glass studio jutting out from the mushroom cap and a curving orange staircase swerving to the sidewalk, puts it into the "Holy what?!" housing hall of fame.

Recognized among his peers for his architectural genius, Brown died in 2008, but his architectural legacy lives on in this magnificent piece of art, both a beloved local landmark and Cincinnati original.

# 85 ST. ROSE CHURCH

## Why does one of the church's tower clocks face the Northern Kentucky shoreline?

With steeple perched atop a clock tower and stretching skyward, the Romanesque-style St. Rose's is the very image of a church one might see pictured in the twilight cityscape of a snow-glittered Christmas card.

Don't let the pretty exterior fool you; this is one hardy church that has survived numerous floods, two fires, and several random acts of vandalism.

A Roman Catholic church in Cincinnati's East End neighborhood, St. Rose's sits dangerously close to the Ohio River; in fact, church and river have a shared history when it comes to flooding that goes back to before the building was even finished.

The parish was founded in 1867, and the church dedicated in 1869. The first recorded flood: 1884. More than sixty floods have followed, including the Big One, the Great Flood of 1937, when the church was swallowed up in eighty feet of water. The church was so impacted by the swelling of the Ohio River that a Flood Gauge was painted on the rear of the building.

Regardless of its waterlogged history, St. Rose's remains a tribute to its German heritage, a warm and welcoming beacon to generations of parishioners, exquisitely beautiful inside with stained-glass windows, brilliant blue dome, and breathtaking statuary, its banks of candles lit for intentions adding a soft glow.

### ST. ROSE CHURCH

**WHAT** Blessed flood benchmark

**WHERE** 2501 Riverside Dr.

**COST** Free

**PRO TIP** Several benches line the riverbank behind St. Rose, a quiet place to sit and enjoy the Ohio River.

strosecincinnati.org

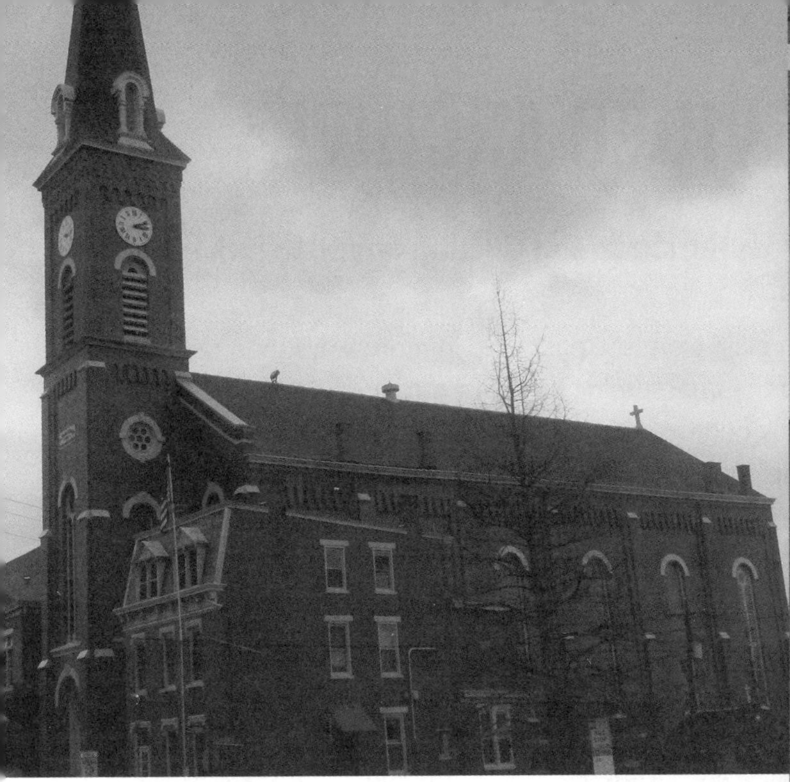

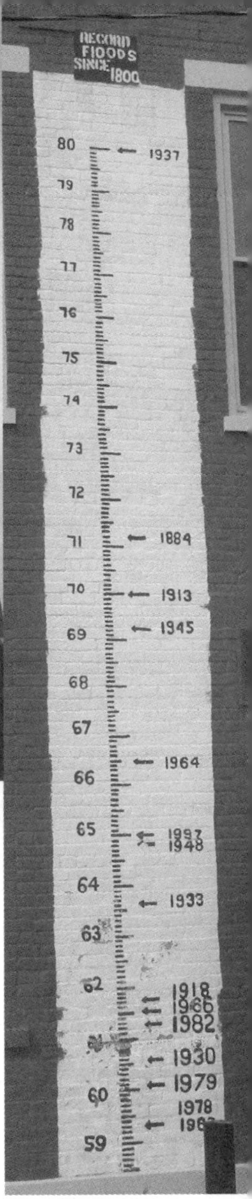


*President William Howard Taft (1909–1913) once visited the children at St. Rose School on train stops from Cincinnati. The old Fulton station was across from the church.* (Inset) *Flood history is recorded right on St. Rose Church. Photo courtesy of John Witt.*

Find the symbol of St. Rose, a Tertiary Dominican who made her living by sewing, in the dome above the main alter. The floral motif weaves thimble, pin cushion, and two needles (one threaded) into its design of two crossed anchors surrounded by a crown of thorns. The organ was installed in 1894 and still has its original hand-painted façade. In the rear of the church the Pieta (which depicts Jesus' body on the lap of Mary after the Crucifixion) is hand-carved of solid wood.

---

The Tower Clock has four faces, one directed south toward the river. It was paid for by those involved in Cincinnati's bustling steamboat building business as well as the citizens of Bellevue, Kentucky.

# 86 THE VIDEO ARCHIVE

## Where does the shadow of Quentin Tarantino lurk in Cincinnati?

Yes, it is a blast from the past (and in more ways than one). Walk into the unassuming brick storefront where the soft-spoken guy behind the counter presents you with a clue to a movie. Search among the VHS tapes (yes, VHS tapes!) along the wall and pull one from its perch. If you've guessed correctly, a door magically slides open to reveal a speakeasy concealed behind it.

Welcome to the Video Archive, an anachronism inspired by the films of Quentin Tarantino and an immersive experience that transports visitors immediately to Moviedom.

Located in Cincinnati's Walnut Hills neighborhood, the intimate and dimly lit bar is a year-round celebration of celluloid, with a particular bent toward indie films and cult classics. The space is geeked up with a photo collage inspired by Uma Thurman's Mia Wallace and a Wurlitzer juke box. Film events with themed décor are the Video Archive's stock-in-trade, like "Yuletide Nightmare" staged in October, when the bar gets a macabre makeover a la Tim Burton's *A Nightmare Before Christmas*.

The bar opens to a patio with a firepit and comfy seating scattered beneath strings of lights. (This is also how you exit the venue; the sliding door entry from the video store is strictly one way.) Just Q'in Barbecue shares the space, so hungry barflies can grab a wood-smoked Goliath sammich or

### THE VIDEO ARCHIVE

**WHAT** Speakeasy bar

**WHERE** 965 E. McMillan St.

**COST** See website

**PRO TIP** During the summer, movies are screened on the Cinema Patio every night, and they take requests.

gorillacinemapresents.com/archive

*The Video Archive rocks a relic-of-the-past vibe with its video store fronting a speakeasy bar and outdoor patio screening movies. Photos courtesy of John Witt.*

a plate of Judas chicken and wash it down with a bourbon-splashed Jackie Brown or fancied-up cognac called the Dmango Unchained.

The occasional celebrity has been known to slip into the speakeasy, and film fans hoping to score a pop culture conquest may find themselves rubbing elbows with Someone Famous. The Video Archive has hosted such screen and stage luminaries as director Kevin Smith (*Clerks, Chasing Amy, Mall Rats*) and the entire Broadway cast of *Something Rotten*, starring Adam Pascal.

---

Downtown's Japanese-style karaoke bar, Tokyo Kitty, is another concept bar from the creators of the Video Archive. Its inspiration: the film *Lost in Translation*. Its symbol: the lucky cat, her paw beckoning your "inner extrovert."

# 87 VENT HAVEN MUSEUM

## How did a museum dedicated to dummies land in Cincinnati?

Visitors from all parts of the globe travel to a quiet residential neighborhood on the Kentucky side of the Ohio River to see the collection of Cincinnati native William Shakespeare Berger. Berger is the founder of Vent Haven Museum, the only museum in the world dedicated to the centuries-old performance art of ventriloquism.

Although not a professional ventriloquist, Berger amassed a staggering number of dummies and puppets over a forty-year period. And not only dummies, but photos, scripts, memorabilia, playbills, posters, recordings, and more. If it was related to ventriloquism, Berger collected it, beginning with a Tommy Baloney figure, his first collection item purchased in 1910 after seeing a ventriloquism performance in New York City during a business trip.

By 1947, Berger's pastime had taken over the garage at his Fort Mitchell home. Fifteen years later, in 1962, he built a second building for the ever-expanding collection. In 1973, Berger's vast collection opened officially to the public. Today, having nearly doubled in size, Vent Haven Museum houses more than nine hundred dummies used by ventriloquists from the nineteenth, twentieth, and twenty-first centuries. The

---

The annual four-day Vent Haven ConVENTion takes place in Northern Kentucky in July. The event features headlining names from the world of ventriloquism, stage shows, open mic sessions, workshops, lectures, Junior Vent University, and massive dealer rooms.

*Vent Haven Museum is the world's only museum dedicated to ventriloquism. Photo used with permission of Vent Haven Museum, Inc.*

## VENT HAVEN MUSEUM

**WHAT** Dummies and dolls

**WHERE** 33 West Maple Ave., Fort Mitchell, KY

**COST** $10 per person donation requested. Open May 1 through September 30. All tours by appointment.

**PRO TIP** Tours are by appointment, but not difficult to schedule. Sweasy (the museum's only employee) gives tours nearly every day of Vent Haven's touring season.

venthaven.org

oldest dummies in the collection date to the 1860s.

According to museum curator/director Lisa Sweasy, every ventriloquist you have ever heard of has visited the museum: Edgar Bergen (whose characters were Charlie McCarthy and Mortimer Snerd), Paul Winchell, Jimmy Nelson, Shari Lewis, Willie Tyler, Jay Johnson, Jeff Dunham, Terry Fator, and Darci Lynne, among others.

Guided tours can last from forty-five minutes to about ninety minutes, depending on visitor interests, and include four puppets that may be handled. All the other dummies and exhibit items are strictly hands-off.

# 88 WALNUT HILLS PRESBYTERIAN CHURCH TOWER

**WALNUT HILLS PRESBYTERIAN CHURCH TOWER**

**WHAT** Stone tower

**WHERE** Corner of William Howard Taft Rd. and Gilbert Ave.

**COST** Free

**PRO TIP** According to the Cincinnati Preservation Association, Cincinnati leads the state of Ohio in listings on the National Register of Historic Places.

cincinnatipreservation.org

## What happened to the church once attached to this tower?

Like a once mighty but long-forgotten stone fortress, the tower rises forlornly at the corner of William Howard Taft Road and Gilbert Avenue, located about a one-minute drive from the Harriet Beecher Stowe House in Cincinnati's historic Walnut Hills neighborhood.

In 2003, the circa 1880s Walnut Hills Presbyterian Church was torn down to make way for the parking lot expansion of the funeral home next door. Preservation groups fought to save the church, but costs to renovate the crumbling structure could have potentially run into the millions. Even its 1980 designation as a landmark on the National Register of Historic Places couldn't save the church. Ultimately, the Cincinnati Preservation Association plunked down one hundred sixty thousand dollars for the tower and surrounding land and the church itself was torn down.

Through its association with the Lane Theological Seminary, the church historically had ties to the Civil War and even beyond, to 1834 and the antislavery debates.

*Even in its urban setting, the church tower evokes images of Rapunzel letting down her hair. Photo courtesy of John Witt.*

The seminary was founded in Cincinnati in 1830, and Rev. Lyman Beecher (Harriet Beecher Stowe's father) was the head of the school between 1832 and 1850. In 1834, the Lane Seminary held an eighteen-day debate on slavery, known as the first public discussion on this topic. The seminary split over the issue of slavery, with the school's board of directors attempting to prohibit students from supporting abolitionism, and enrollment declined.

Should restoration ever take place, it will be up to the tower to narrate the history not only of the church but also of those long-ago antislavery debates. Plans to do exactly that were hatched years ago and included adding bells, landscaping, and permanent exhibits; however, as is the case for so many worthy structures, funding has not allowed plans to proceed.

For now, the spireless tower with its Gothic windows and arched doorways awaits an uncertain future, but what a fabulous photo-op.

---

Abolitionist and fiery orator Lyman Beecher graduated from Yale University in 1797 and was ordained a Presbyterian minister in 1799. He moved his family to Cincinnati in 1832 to serve as president of the Lane Theological Seminary.

# 89 TROLLEY PARK

**What does a streetcar from the early nineteenth century have to do with a playground?**

There is a little pocket of paradise in Park Hills, perfect for reading a book, enjoying a quiet lunch, or watching the kids climb and romp at the playground.

Sitting not far from the entrance to Devou Park is Trolley Park, one of the most splendid small-town parks anywhere. Lushly planted with a variety of trees and shrubs, it has a water fountain burbling over rocks, plants spilling over with colorful blooms, and lampposts and statuary adding charm to the grounds.

Curving stone benches bracket a circular brick patio stamped with "Trolley Park" and an image of the No. 19 Covington/Cincinnati streetcar. The windows in the stone shelters are made of colored glass and depict a trolley (coming and going). A garden arbor arches over an entrance with drinking fountain nearby.

Immaculately maintained from a thick, trimmed lawn to the children's playground equipment standing on a soft bed of mulch, the park is an

## TROLLEY PARK

**WHAT** Private pocket park

**WHERE** 1101 Amsterdam Rd., Park Hills, KY

**COST** Free

**PRO TIP** Parking is available at Trolley Park near the children's playground.

Visitors to Behringer-Crawford in Devou Park can't miss the *Kentucky* parked inside its entrance. Restored to its original look, the streetcar comes to life with a push of the button to relate stories about the passengers onboard.

(Above) *The children's playground at Trolley Park.* (Left) *An image of a streetcar is depicted in the windows at Trolley Park. Photos courtesy of John Witt.*

irresistible draw for young families, picnickers, and those simply moved to pull over to stop and smell the bougainvillea.

The park was named in honor of the bustling trolley line that ran through the area until the early 1950s, connecting Park Hills to Cincinnati, Covington, and other towns in Northern Kentucky. Devou Park was a popular destination for trolley riders, and passengers would disembark the trolley near the now-historic stone buildings that once sheltered commuters at either end of Trolley Park.

The *Kentucky* car was one of the streetcars that served this area. Built in the 1890s, it was a party car with a beautiful interior that revelers could rent for weddings and other special occasions. During its heyday, as Park Hills was burgeoning as a city, it played host to many a grand event. The *Kentucky* made its last trip in 1950.

# INDEX